Strange Roads and Forbidden Paths

Strange Roads and Forbidden Paths

Avoiding Apostasy in the Latter Days

Richard G. Moore

CFI
Springville, Utah

ISBN 978-1-59955-211-8

Published by CFI, an imprint of Cedar Fort, Inc., 2373 W. 700 S., Springville, UT 84663
Distributed by Cedar Fort, Inc., www.cedarfort.com

LIBRARY OF CONGRESS CATALOGING-IN-PUBLICATION DATA
Moore, Richard G., 1952-
Strange roads and forbidden paths : avoiding apostasy in the latter days /
Richard G. Moore.
p. cm.
ISBN 978-1-59955-211-8 (alk. paper)
1. Apostasy--Church of Jesus Christ of Latter-day Saints. 2.
Apostasy--Mormon Church. 3. Church of Jesus Christ of Latter-day
Saints--Doctrines. 4. Mormon Church--Doctrines. I. Title.

BX8643.G74M66 2008
230'.9332--dc22

2008026828

Cover design by Angela Olsen
Cover design © 2008 by Lyle Mortimer
Edited and typeset by Melissa J. Caldwell

Printed in the United States of America

10 9 8 7 6 5 4 3 2 1

Printed on acid-free paper

for lani

Other books by Richard G. Moore

12 Keys to Developing Spiritual Maturity

Contents

Acknowledgments

Thanks to Alonzo Gaskill, John Thompson, Gary Perras, and Lani Moore for reading all or parts of the manuscript and making suggestions for valuable and needed changes. Thanks to Melissa Caldwell, a great editor and very nice person. Thanks to the good people at Cedar Fort, Inc. And a special thanks to my lovely wife, Lani, for her encouragement and support.

INTRODUCTION

Chapter eight of 1 Nephi gives us an account of Lehi's dream of the tree of life. Some people in the dream, such as Lehi's eldest sons, Laman and Lemuel, refused to approach the tree, while others started toward the tree but were lost in a great mist of darkness. Multitudes of people tried to make their way to the great and spacious building, but many were drowned in the depths of the fountain, and others were lost from Lehi's view, wandering in strange roads.

Among the numberless hosts that Lehi saw pressing toward the tree, there were many who "caught hold of the end of the rod of iron" (1 Nephi 8:24) and either clinging to or holding fast to that rod, made their way to the tree. However, among those who arrived safely at the tree and even partook of the fruit were individuals who "fell away into forbidden paths and were lost" (1 Nephi 8:28).

For someone to partake of the gospel of Jesus Christ by receiving sacred ordinances and making covenants with the Lord and then rejecting or walking away from inspired truths to follow "forbidden paths" is an act of apostasy. I differentiate between people who do acts of apostasy and apostates in the same manner I consider people who are going through the process of conversion and those who have become true converts.

In other words, a person who is being taught by the missionaries, praying, and reading the scriptures is on the road to conversion but will only become a convert if he stays on the path and presses forward. In like manner, a member of the Church who criticizes Church leaders or doctrines or is guilty of serious sin without attempting to repent is committing acts of apostasy and can become an apostate if he stays on that path and presses forward. Apostasy is just as much a progression as conversion—each has varying degrees.

God established His Church on the earth in the days of Adam and Eve, and whenever God's children rejected or strayed from the authority and teachings of His Church, they were in a state of apostasy. When Jesus Christ came to the earth during His mortal ministry, it was necessary for Him to reestablish His Father's true Church on the earth. The people responsible for abandoning or altering Christ's Church after His death and resurrection were apostates, and they caused the Great Apostasy. The fact that there was a Great Apostasy is the very reason for how the Lord responded to Joseph Smith's prayer. When Joseph Smith asked God which church he should join, the Lord told him that he "must join none of them, for they were all wrong" (JS—History 1:19).

This is not to say that *all* of the teachings of these other churches are wrong. Of course, other churches have many truths. These truths came from God. Churches that believe the Bible to be God's word have access to the truths found in that sacred record. Those who believe in Jesus Christ are correct in having faith in Him as our Lord and Savior. Some churches even believe some of the events of the Restoration and may have the Book of Mormon and other revelations received by Joseph Smith. But where false doctrines and traditions have been added to the truths revealed by prophets, or where God's truth has been altered or removed by man, then error has become an element of that church and they are, at least in part, wrong or in an apostasy.

Personal apostasy will continue to take place throughout the latter days until the Second Coming of Christ and even after the Millennium. It is my belief that each of us has the capability of falling into forbidden paths because in our fallen, mortal condition, each carries the seeds of apostasy.

What can we do to keep ourselves and our families safe from apostasy during this final dispensation before the return of Jesus Christ? The purpose of this book is to give an overview of apostasy that has existed on the earth since the beginning and to alert Church members to the dangers of apostasy that exist today. We will explore issues that can lead to apostasy, examine case studies of apostates since the Restoration, and discover ways of protecting ourselves from becoming victims of apostasy.

I have based my findings on scriptural research and studying the writings of latter-day prophets, seers, and revelators. I have also drawn from personal experiences and observations. Clearly, I do not speak for The Church of Jesus Christ of Latter-day Saints. I hope that my opinions are valid and of worth, but in the end, they are simply my opinions. Truths found in this book come from the Lord through inspired prophets and leaders and by the whisperings of the Spirit. I am responsible for any errors.

1

Apostasy in Former Dispensations

Apostasy in one form or another has existed in every generation since man appeared on the earth. Adam and Eve were taught gospel truths by the voice of the Lord, by angelic visitation, and through the gift of the Holy Ghost. Our first parents then "made all things known unto their sons and their daughters" (Moses 5:12). Thus, the children of Adam and Eve were taught the gospel. However, "Satan came among them, saying: I am also a son of God; and he commanded them, saying: Believe it not; and they believed it not, and they loved Satan more than God. And men began from that time forth to be carnal, sensual, and devilish" (Moses 5:13). Apostasy had appeared in the world.

We could go back even farther than the time of Adam and Eve to the days of our premortal existence. While we lived as spirit children in the presence of our Father in Heaven, apostasy took place in the form of open rebellion when a third part of the hosts of heaven followed Lucifer, the archangel of apostasy. Their apostasy cost them their first estate and caused them to be cast out.

Examples of Apostasy in the Old Testament

We learn from the book of Moses that after the fall of Adam and Eve, the couple was driven out of the Garden of Eden and began to have children. "And Adam knew his wife, and she bare unto him sons and daughters, and they began to multiply and replenish the earth" (Moses

5:2). Adam and Eve were righteous parents and taught the gospel to their sons and daughters, but some of their children refused to believe the eternal truths taught to them by their parents.

The LDS Bible Dictionary states that because the biblical record we have is incomplete, many "have regarded Cain as the eldest son of Adam. However, latter-day revelation tells us that Adam and Eve had many sons and daughters before Cain was born."[1] Although Cain was not the first child of Adam and Eve to apostatize, he is the first example where some detail of his apostasy is given. When Cain was born, Eve said, "I have gotten a man from the Lord; wherefore he may not reject his words" (Moses 5:16). Eve appears to be expressing her heartfelt desire that this child might not fall away from the gospel path as some of her other children possibly had done. Cain was taught the gospel by his righteous parents. According to Brigham Young, "Cain conversed with his God every day, and knew all about the plan of creating this earth, for his father told him."[2]

From the Prophet Joseph Smith we learn that Cain was authorized to offer the sacrifice required of Adam and his posterity.[3] Cain was a priesthood holder. But his offering to the Lord was not made in righteousness. Cain rejected the teachings of his parents and he "loved Satan more than God" (Moses 5:18).

Even after Cain made an unrighteous offering under the direction of Satan, he still had an opportunity to repent and return to God. The Lord said to Cain, "If thou doest well, thou shalt be accepted. And if thou doest not well, sin lieth at the door, and Satan desireth to have thee; and except thou shalt hearken unto my commandments, I will deliver thee up" (Moses 5:23). Cain did not respond to the mercy of God and because of his pride, greed, and hatred he "listened not any more to the voice of the Lord" (Moses 5:26).

Cain sealed his own fate by rejecting the Lord. Joseph Fielding Smith taught, "As far as Cain is concerned, the information given is definite that he became Perdition."[4] This was not a one-man apostasy. We are told in the Pearl of Great Price that "Adam and his wife mourned before the Lord, because of Cain *and his brethren*." And Cain took a wife and "*they* loved Satan more than God" (Moses 5:27–28; emphasis added).

Apostasy in the Days of Noah

Beginning with Cain and his brethren, apostasy continued among many of Adam's descendants until we arrive at the days of Noah when "the wickedness of men had become great in the earth; and every man was lifted up in the imagination of the thoughts of his heart, *being only evil continually*" (Moses 8:22, emphasis added). Joseph Fielding Smith wrote, "There have been times when the gospel has been taken from men because of their transgression. Such was the case in the days of Noah."[5] The City of Enoch was removed from the face of the earth prior to the days of Noah. During the time of Noah some righteous people died prior to the flood, such as Methuselah and Lamech, while others were translated. In vision Enoch saw that after his city of Zion was taken off the earth and prior to the flood, angels would descend "out of heaven, bearing testimony of the Father and Son; and the Holy Ghost fell on many, and they were caught up by the powers of heaven into Zion" (Moses 7:27).

It appears that the only righteous people left on earth were Noah and his family. The flood cleansed the earth of wickedness, placing the unrighteous in the spirit world to provide for them a better chance for repentance, and leaving Noah's righteous family to begin again the process of bringing Heavenly Father's children to earth to receive physical bodies.

Even with this new beginning, it did not take long for apostasy to appear again on the earth. From the Tower of Babel to the end of the Old Testament, we witness a series of apostasies culminating in an apostate condition that would last through the intertestamental period until the mortal ministry of Jesus. Brigham Young University scholar M. Catherine Thomas wrote, "These Pharisees who sought Jesus' life were the descendants of that apostasy that thrived in Old Testament times and into the succeeding period."[6] Because of the repeated apostasy of the Israelites during Old Testament times, it is easy to see example after example of apostasy in that ancient record. The Old Testament appears to be a story of the successes and failures of the children of God to follow their Father in Heaven.

Examples of Apostasy in the Book of Mormon

The Book of Mormon begins in a setting of apostasy. Nephi tells us that there were many prophets in Jerusalem warning the people that if they did not repent, they would either be destroyed or led into captivity. Lehi was called of God to be one of those prophets, admonishing the people to give up their abominations and return to God. "And it came to pass that the Jews did mock him because of the things which he testified of them; for he truly testified of their wickedness and their abominations; and . . . they were angry with him; yea, even as with the prophets of old, whom they had cast out, and stoned, and slain; and they also sought his life, that they might take it away" (1 Nephi 1:19–20).

Lehi was instructed by God to take his family away from the Jerusalem area and flee into the wilderness. Lehi escaped from the apostates of Jerusalem, but he could not escape apostasy. His own sons, Laman and Lemuel, along with some of Ishmael's family, rejected the Lord's counsel and opposed Lehi and the faithful members of his family.

Apostasy in the Book of Mormon resulted in a division in this family and created two groups of people that were often at odds with each other. And although it is obvious at the first of the Book of Mormon that the Nephites are true followers of God and the Lamanites are the apostates, the situation does not stay clear-cut for long. The Nephites were plagued with dissenters from the faith, some going over to the side of the Lamanites, others staying among the Nephites and causing greater problems. On the other hand, numerous Lamanites converted to the truth of the gospel of Jesus Christ, rejecting the apostate teachings of their ancestors and becoming fellow citizens with the Saints of God.

Zoramites

One of the better-known examples of apostasy in the Book of Mormon is the Zoramites. These people were Nephites raised with gospel truths that had rejected the truth for apostate doctrines. Their leader, Zoram, "was leading the hearts of the people to bow down to dumb idols" (Alma 31:1). Many Zoramites still claimed to believe in God. They built synagogues and attended weekly worship services, but they had perverted the ways of the Lord to such an extent that when Alma and his missionary companions witnessed a Zoramite worship service "they were astonished beyond all measure" (Alma 31:19).

The synagogue had a Rameumptom or "prayer stand" where each individual attending the meeting would stand with stretched forth hands and recite in a loud voice the following prayer:

> Holy, holy God; we believe that thou art God, and we believe that thou art holy, and that thou wast a spirit, and that thou art a spirit, and that thou wilt be a spirit forever.
>
> Holy God, we believe that thou hast separated us from our brethren; and we do not believe in the tradition of our brethren, which was handed down to them by the childishness of their fathers; but we believe that thou hast elected us to be thy holy children; and also thou hast made it known unto us that there shall be no Christ.
>
> But thou art the same yesterday, today, and forever; and thou hast elected us that we shall be saved, whilst all around us are elected to be cast by thy wrath down to hell; for the which holiness, O God, we thank thee; and we also thank thee that thou hast elected us, that we may not be led away after the foolish traditions of our brethren, which doth bind them down to a belief of Christ, which doth lead their hearts to wander far from thee, our God.
>
> And again we thank thee, O God, that we are a chosen and a holy people. Amen. (Alma 31:15–18)

These Zoramites had apostatized from the Church of Christ, but to salve their consciences they had created a type of religion where they could profess belief in God and even have a token weekly religious service. They determined that the God they worshiped had chosen them to be saved while all others would be damned. Because they had been "chosen to be saved," they had no other obligations or requirements for their salvation. "Now, after the people had all offered up thanks after this manner, they returned to their homes, never speaking of their God again until they had assembled themselves together again to the holy stand" the next time they attended a church service (Alma 31:23).

Alma observed that these supposedly religious Zoramites "were a wicked and a perverse people; yea, he saw that their hearts were set upon gold, and upon silver, and upon all manner of fine goods. Yea, and he also saw that their hearts were lifted up unto great boasting, in their pride" (Alma 31:24–25).

Apostasy after the Savior's Visit

A most alarming example of apostasy in the Book of Mormon is found in 4 Nephi. Within a few years after the visit of the resurrected Savior to the Nephites and Lamanites who had survived the great destruction accompanying the crucifixion of Christ, "the people were all converted to the Lord" (4 Nephi 1:2). A Zion society was created where "there was no contention in the land, because of the love of God which did dwell in the hearts of the people. And there were no envyings, nor strifes, nor tumults, nor whoredoms, nor lyings, nor murders, nor any manner of lasciviousness; and *surely there could not be a happier people among all the people who had been created by the hand of God*" (4 Nephi 1:15–16, emphasis added).

This ideal society existed for more than one hundred fifty years. One might wonder why anyone living in such a blessed situation would ever want anything different. But we see in 4 Nephi 1:20 that a small part of the people revolted from the Church. Not many years later there began to be pride, worldliness, and class conflict in their society. And "there were many churches which professed to know the Christ, and yet they did deny the more parts of his gospel" (4 Nephi 1:27).

Acts of apostasy had begun to destroy the Nephite civilization. Other churches arose that denied Christ entirely and persecuted the humble followers of Jesus. Mormon tells us that many of these were not people who had simply dwindled in unbelief but had willfully rebelled against the gospel of Christ (4 Nephi 1:38). This condition of apostasy continued its downward spiral until all the righteous believers were destroyed and only the unbelievers remained.

Examples of Apostasy in the New Testament

The New Testament begins during an era of apostasy. Part of Jesus

Christ's mortal ministry was to restore the fulness of the gospel to the earth—a fulness that had been lost because of apostasy. There were still righteous people among the house of Israel in the Holy Land of the New Testament. Zacharias is an example of the righteous priests who still served God during that time. Many righteous men and women lived in Judea, people like Elizabeth, Simeon at the temple, Anna, the shepherds who were visited by angels on the night of the Savior's birth, and all of the people who loved and followed Jesus Christ when he walked the earth as a mortal. There were good men among the many scribes, Pharisees, and Sadducees. Yet in the highest levels of the religious leadership of Israel during that era, there also existed dreadful apostasy.

The Savior warned the people to beware of the doctrine of these apostate Pharisees and Sadducees. The Prince of Peace Himself described these men as vipers, hypocrites, blind, and "whited sepulchres, which indeed appear beautiful outward, but are within full of dead men's bones, and of all uncleanness" (Matthew 23:27).

It was this group of apostate Israelite religious leaders who urged Pilate to have Jesus Christ put to death. Concerning these wicked religious leaders, the Book of Mormon prophet Jacob tells us that they were the "more wicked part of the world" and at that time there was "none other nation on earth that would crucify their God" (2 Nephi 10:3).[7]

Judas Iscariot

Judas Iscariot is the model for New Testament apostasy. President Gordon B. Hinckley has referred to Judas as "the great betrayer."[8] His apostasy and treachery appears to be a result of his greed and disloyalty. Judas Iscariot was called by the Savior to be one of His apostles. As a member of the Twelve, Judas spent much time with Jesus, heard His teachings, witnessed numerous miracles, and received the priesthood. As an apostle, he was a special witness of Jesus Christ. Luke records that Satan entered into Judas Iscariot, and he betrayed the Lord for thirty pieces of silver. It would be difficult to imagine anyone falling further than Judas Iscariot. President Thomas S. Monson wrote, "[Judas Iscariot] commenced his ministry as an apostle of the Lord. He ended it a traitor."[9]

The apostasy of many of the Israelite religious rulers during New Testament times and the personal apostasy of Judas Iscariot are clear examples of apostasy during that era. There are less dramatic instances of what might be considered acts of apostasy in the New Testament. When Jesus had concluded his Bread of Life Sermon, many of his followers said, "This is an hard saying; who can hear it?" (John 6:60).

Some people were willing to follow Jesus to an extent. They were willing to be healed, willing to be fed in a miraculous manner, even willing to accept some of the teachings of Jesus. But during the Bread of Life Sermon, many either did not understand what He was teaching or else they refused to accept Jesus as the Messiah. John records, "From that time many of his disciples went back, and walked no more with him" (John 6:66). If a disciple—by definition a believer, supporter, and follower—refuses to continue to follow the Savior, then he has forsaken the path of discipleship and has entered the road of apostasy.

New Testament Prophecies concerning the Great Apostasy

In addition to writing about the apostasy of their own time, the authors of the New Testament manuscripts also prophesied of a wide scale apostasy that was about to happen. This Great Apostasy had also been foreseen and noted by some Old Testament prophets. In vision Isaiah saw a darkness covering the earth and a "gross darkness" enveloping the people (Isaiah 60:2). The prophet Amos wrote, "Behold, the days come, saith the Lord God, that I will send a famine in the land, not a famine of bread, nor a thirst for water, but of hearing the words of the Lord: And they shall wander from sea to sea, and from the north even to the east, they shall run to and fro to seek the word of the Lord, and shall not find it" (Amos 8:11–12). The word of the Lord in its fulness would not be found because of the sweeping nature of the Great Apostasy. This would be a universal apostasy from the Church established by Jesus. The fulness of the gospel of Jesus Christ would be lost to the inhabitants of the earth.

Jesus Christ and New Testament apostles not only foresaw the coming of the Great Apostasy, but some also lived to witness the beginnings of the abandonment of gospel truths and the demise of the true

Church in the meridian of time. The Savior warned of false Christs and false prophets who would deceive some of His followers. The apostle Paul said to a group of elders who had met with him in Miletus, "For I know this, that after my departing shall grievous wolves enter in among you, not sparing the flock. Also of your own selves shall men arise, speaking perverse things, to draw away disciples after them" (Acts 20:29–30). He spoke of apostates arising from within the Church trying to lead believers astray.

To the troubled Thessalonians who had been hearing rumors and false doctrines about the second coming of Christ, Paul wrote: "Let no man deceive you by any means: for that day shall not come, except there come a falling away first, and that man of sin be revealed, the son of perdition; Who opposeth and exalteth himself above all that is called God, or that is worshipped; so that he as God sitteth in the temple of God, shewing himself that he is God" (2 Thessalonians 2:3–4). Speaking of this verse and particularly about Satan sitting in the temple of God, Elder James E. Talmage wrote:

> By the temple of God the apostle could not well mean the temple of Jerusalem, because that, he knew, would be destroyed within a few years. After the death of Christ, the temple of Jerusalem is never called the temple of God; and if, at any time, they make mention of the house or temple of God, they mean the church in general or every particular believer. Whoever will consult 1 Corinthians 3:16, 17; 2 Corinthians 6:16; 1 Timothy 3:15; Revelation 3:12, will want no examples to prove that under the gospel dispensation, the temple of God is the Church of Christ; and the man of sin's sitting implies his ruling and presiding there.[10]

From this we should understand that the Great Apostasy did not completely destroy the entity that was the Church, but because the authority was lost the organization that remained was no longer the Church of Jesus Christ. The shell would still be there, but without the authority of the priesthood the heart and soul of the Church was gone, leaving an opening into which Satan would enter. There were still good people who believed in Christ, but little by little the adversary removed true doctrine while managing to convince many of the people that all was well with the Church. Paul saw that very thing happening when he prophesied that people would "turn away their ears from the truth, and shall be turned unto fables" (2 Timothy 4:4).

Peter said to some former dispensation Saints that "there shall be false teachers among you, who privily shall bring in damnable heresies, even denying the Lord that bought them" (2 Peter 2:1). Jude was not speaking of a future day, but of things that had already happened when he wrote, "For there are certain men crept in unawares, . . . ungodly men, turning the grace of our God into lasciviousness, and denying the only Lord God, and our Lord Jesus Christ" (Jude 1:4). In the version of the Bible known as the Jerusalem Bible, the words "crept in unawares" are translated as "infiltrated." Wicked men had infiltrated the Church of Christ and were altering doctrine and leading people astray from within.

John also saw the beginnings of apostasy within the Church of Christ. He reported that "even now, are there many antichrists; . . . They went out from us, but they were not of us; for if they had been of us, they would no doubt have continued with us: but they went out" (1 John 2:18–19).

The term *anti-Christ* is interesting in that there are several possible definitions. Modern English usage of the word *anti* would suggest opposition, being against, or being hostile toward. This makes sense when we think of an anti-Christ as one who fights against Christ or who is opposed to the teachings of or a belief in Jesus Christ. However, from the Greek, another treatment of the word *anti* means "instead of" or "in the place of." This could suggest that an anti-Christ was an imposter or one who assumed the guise of a savior, one who was trying to take the place of Christ. In a sense, anyone or anything that promises salvation or the right path to follow, which is not of Jesus Christ, would be a false Christ or an anti-Christ.

After the death of Jesus Christ and His apostles in the eastern hemisphere and the destruction of the Nephites in the western hemisphere, the Great Apostasy swept over the world, and the earth was plunged into darkness. Apostasy reigned and priesthood ordinances and blessings were withheld from mortals on the earth for many years until the Restoration.

NOTES

1. Bible Dictionary, "Cain," 628.
2. Brigham Young, in *Journal of Discourses,* 2:142.
3. Smith, *Teachings of the Prophet Joseph Smith,* 169.
4. Smith, *Answers to Gospel Questions,* 2:171.
5. Smith, *Doctrines of Salvation,* 1:162.
6. M. Catherine Thomas, "From Malachi to John the Baptist: The Dynamics of Apostasy," in *Studies in Scripture: 1 Kings to Malachi,* 473.
7. Also see *Teachings of the Prophet Joseph Smith,* 328, where Joseph Smith is recorded to have said, "This generation is as corrupt as the generation of the Jews that crucified Christ; and if He were here today, and should preach the same doctrine He did then, they would put Him to death."
8. Gordon B. Hinckley, "Loyalty," *Ensign,* May 2003, 60.
9. Thomas S. Monson, "Finishers Wanted," *Ensign,* July 1972, 68.
10. Talmage, *The Great Apostasy,* 148.

2

Apostasy in the Latter-day Dispensation

We have seen examples of apostasy from previous dispensations, and it is with certainty that we can find all manner of apostasy during the dispensation of the fulness of times. In fact, being the last days of his power, Satan can be expected to put forth great effort to stop the growth and progress of the kingdom of God.

The restoration of the fulness of the gospel of Jesus Christ began in 1820 when a fourteen-year-old boy prayed to find out which church was God's true church. In the years that followed, the young Joseph Smith received revelation upon revelation; translated an ancient record into the Book of Mormon; and officially organized the Church on April 6, 1830. After many years of absence the kingdom of God was again upon the earth. The fledgling church began to grow, and soon hundreds and thousands entered the waters of baptism based on their faith in Christ and His Church as restored through the Prophet Joseph.

Like every other dispensation, there were those who united with the true Church of Jesus Christ, only to later rebel against what they once considered to be true. Whether abandoning religion entirely, joining another church, starting their own religion, or fighting against the restored gospel, these dissenters committed acts of apostasy as they traveled down that forbidden path and some became full-fledged apostates.

Apostasy in Our Day

I personally became aware of contemporary apostasy from The Church of Jesus Christ of Latter-day Saints when I was very young. I discovered that my next-door neighbor had been a member of the Church but had been excommunicated for teaching and practicing false doctrines. My parents would not go into detail about his situation, and it wasn't until after my mission that I discovered he had been a polygamist.

My neighbor was a very religious man who studied the scriptures, discussed religion constantly with people in the neighborhood, and even wrote a number of doctrinal books. He believed in the restoration of the gospel through Joseph Smith. I remember the old pictures with oval frames of Joseph Smith and Brigham Young that hung on his wall. But he also believed that John Taylor was the last president of the Church that was truly a prophet of God. He believed that there had been a general apostasy among both leaders and the rank and file of the Latter-day Saints. He maintained that there were only a few stalwarts that had remained true to what Joseph Smith had restored.

In addition to my neighbor and the hush-hush circumstances that my parents kept from my siblings and me, there was another Church-related mystery that puzzled me as a youth. Perched on a hillside visible from the home where I was raised was a white stair-step building that locals called the Dream Mine.

I didn't know the history of the Dream Mine until I was older. All I knew was that my parents and my friends' parents told us not to go near the mine because it was private property. We reasoned, "What property in town isn't private property?" Our parents had never mentioned to stay away from any other specific place. Our interest was piqued, but most of us did our best to stay away from the Dream Mine.

When I was older I became more curious about the mine and did some research into its history. The story begins a few years after the Manifesto in 1890 and a few years prior to Lorenzo Snow receiving the "tithing" revelation in St. George. The Church was still suffering from the tremendous financial burden brought about by the anti-polygamy laws of the 1880s. In 1894 a Utah County man said that an angel visited him several nights in succession. The angel told the man that in a nearby hill he would find chambers filled with Nephite records, artifacts, and a vast treasure of Nephite gold. This discovery would bring the Church out of financial bondage and prepare it for the Millennium.

The story encompasses several years and includes claims of visitations from the Three Nephites, Moses, and deceased latter-day prophets. Hundreds of people invested in the mine by purchasing stock, and at least three workers were killed while working at the mine. Official statements from the First Presidency of the Church warned people about getting involved with business ventures based on the revelation of others. Over fifty years after the whole thing began, the man who originally claimed he had received the revelation lost his membership in the Church.

I have just given two examples of apostasy within my little community. However, more apostasy exists during our day than most members of the Church are aware. Organizations and churches that began in apostasy to the restoration are more numerous than most people know. One writer, who has for years kept track of the various church organizations that trace their roots back to the Prophet Joseph Smith, recently wrote, "Over the intervening 150 or so years since Joseph's death, there have been at least 400 different expressions of the little church that began so humbly with a few baptisms in New York and Pennsylvania in 1829 and 1830."[1]

Referring to the various break-off groups as "different expressions" of the restored gospel, that same author claims that it would be folly "for any one of the groups to claim the others were or are apostates" and "a claim of apostasy from a single, unified institution is challenged by the facts of history."[2] I suppose this is the same argument that orthodox Christianity uses to explain why there are so many different denominations or versions of Christ's original church. It makes no sense to say the groups that strayed from the church organized by Jesus are simply different expressions of His Church. Rejecting the truths Jesus taught and the authority He established resulted in the Great Apostasy.

Historical interpretations of what took place prior to and following the death of the Prophet and Patriarch in 1844 do not determine who is right and who is wrong. One of the reasons that so-called orthodox Christianity rejects the churches of the restoration is that "historically" they do not trace their roots to the time of the early Christian fathers.

What we are talking about is authority, priesthood keys, saving ordinances, true doctrine, and the mind and will of God. And because "God is not the author of confusion" (1 Corinthians 14:33), it would make much more sense for each group to proclaim its place as Christ's only true church, rather than concluding that all of the restoration churches, with differing doctrines and beliefs, are right together.

As Latter-day Saints, we do take a bold stand in declaring that The Church of Jesus Christ of Latter-day Saints is God's kingdom here on the earth and is *the* true church. Clearly, this will not win us any popularity contests with those outside of our faith. Our declaration of truth should not be made with arrogance, but with an almost overwhelming sense of responsibility to share the gospel we have with all of God's children. We send missionaries throughout the world with the message of salvation. As Elder Boyd K. Packer stated at the October 2005 general conference of the Church, "Each can receive assurance which comes through inspiration and testifies that Jesus is the Christ, the Son of God, that The Church of Jesus Christ of Latter-day Saints is just as He declared it to be, 'the only true and living church upon the face of the whole earth' (D&C 1:30)."[3]

That said, I maintain that there is a difference between apostates and those who belong to what began as apostate organizations. Most of the people today who belong to groups that broke away from the Church cannot be apostates in the sense that they never were part of the original church restored by the Prophet Joseph Smith in the latter days. They have not taken upon themselves covenants made at baptism or in the holy temple. I do not question their sincerity or their faith, but I do question the veracity of the organizations to which they belong.

I have known a number of people who are members of these other restoration churches, and I know them to be very good people. I believe they are sincerely trying to follow God and are only limited by not having a fulness of the gospel. Like almost all churches, they have the truth in part. I believe that the hearts of many of these people are right before God, and I trust the Lord when He says, "Behold such shall be reclaimed" (D&C 50:7).

When I speak of apostates, I am also not referring to someone being less active in our Church or even those members who want nothing to do with the Church. I am talking about Latter-day Saints and former Latter-day Saints who are in open rebellion against the Church.

What Is Considered Apostasy in Our Time?

English dictionaries may define *apostasy* as abandoning one's faith or belief, or forsaking one's religion. Because we as members of the Church believe that there is only one true and living church on the face of the earth, we would not see leaving any other religion as apostasy. The apostasy we speak of is to rebel against truth—God's truth. Elder Dallin H. Oaks wrote:

> For purposes of church discipline, the Church currently defines apostasy as (1) repeatedly acting in clear, open, and deliberate public opposition to the Church or its leaders; (2) persisting in teaching as church doctrine information that is not church doctrine, after being corrected by one's bishop or higher authority; or (3) continuing to follow the teachings of apostate cults (such as those that advocate plural marriage) after being corrected by one's bishop or higher authority. Total inactivity in the Church or merely attending another church does not constitute apostasy.[4]

Also consider the definition of *apostate* found in the *Encyclopedia of Mormonism:*

> Members of the Church vary in their levels of participation or belief. Latter-day Saints who have seriously contravened or ignored cardinal Church teachings (publicly or privately) are considered apostates, whether or not they have officially left the Church or affiliated with another religion. By not participating in Church meetings one is not considered apostate. However, when individuals ask to have their names removed from Church records, policy requires

> such requests to be honored. A Church disciplinary procedure may be held for any member who violates important commandments and "will not repent" (Mosiah 26:32; D&C 42:28). Open repudiation of the Church, its leaders, and teachings is one ground for excommunication.[5]

The Church has written policies for handling situations when official discipline is deemed necessary. Only God can truly know the heart of a person and the situation that led to an individual's actions. Just as only God knows the difference between the hearts of those who simply have membership in the Church compared to those who are truly converted, He also knows and recognizes the differences between those guilty of acts of apostasy and those who truly have become apostates.

In the same way that following the strait and narrow path is a process whereby God's children can eventually receive exaltation, the wide gate and broad way "that leadeth to destruction" is also a process (Matthew 7:13). There are degrees of apostasy, but the road that leads to total rebellion can begin with little indiscretions. Disobedience to any of God's commandments could be considered an act of apostasy because it is a rejection of or turning away from certain truths.

In our weak and fallen state, we are all guilty of disobedience to one degree or another. However, willful disobedience is much more serious than straying in ignorance, being deceived, or slipping in a moment of weakness. Willful disobedience puts an individual in open opposition to God, rejecting His counsel and defying His laws. Elder Bruce R. McConkie wrote:

> It follows that if members of the Church believe false doctrines; if they accept false educational theories; if they fall into the practices and abominations of the sectarians; if they use tea, coffee, tobacco or liquor; if they fail to pay an honest tithing; if they find fault with the Lord's anointed; if they play cards; if they do anything contrary to the standards of personal righteousness required by the gospel—*then to that extent they are in personal apostasy and need to repent.*[6]

According to Elder McConkie, a person can be guilty of acts of apostasy to a certain extent if he rejects any doctrine of the kingdom for some other belief, ideology, or false doctrine. Again, there are varying degrees of seriousness of acts of apostasy.

We cannot be guilty of apostasy for not knowing or understanding a gospel truth that the Lord has not yet revealed. And while not knowing a gospel doctrine that has been revealed may be evidence of a lack of study, it could hardly be considered apostasy. What teacher in the Church has not been guilty of accidentally teaching something that was incorrect? The Prophet Joseph Smith said, "It does not prove that a man is not a good man because he errs in doctrine."[7]

If a person who believes or teaches false doctrines has been corrected by one in authority, and afterwards still persists in teaching or advocating these false principles, then he has started down the road to apostasy. This is not to say that a Church member cannot have an honest difference of opinion with a Church leader without becoming an apostate. But let it be known that this is a precarious position. Satan thrives on contention and pride, both of which are very real possibilities in such circumstances. George Q. Cannon, an apostle and counselor in the First Presidency, wrote:

> A friend came to us this morning to question us respecting our views concerning apostasy. He wished to know whether we had said that we considered an honest difference of opinion between a member of the Church and the authorities of the Church apostasy, as he said, we had been credited with having made a statement to this effect. We replied that we had not stated that an honest difference of opinion between a member of the Church and the authorities constituted apostasy; for we could conceive of a man honestly differing in opinion from the authorities of the Church and yet not be an apostate; but we could not conceive of a man publishing those differences of opinion, and seeking by arguments, sophistry and special pleading to enforce them upon the people to produce division and strife, and to place the acts and counsels of the authorities of the Church, if possible, in a wrong light, and not be an apostate; for such conduct was apostasy as we understood the term. We further said that *while a man might honestly differ in opinion from the authorities through a want of understanding, he had to be exceedingly careful how he acted*

> *in relation to such differences, or the adversary would take advantage of him and he would soon become imbued with the spirit of apostasy, and be found fighting against God and the authority which He had placed here to govern His Church.*[8]

Effects of Apostasy

One of the effects of apostasy is a loss of knowledge of truth and light. Speaking to Zeezrom, the contentious lawyer of the Zoramites, Alma said:

> It is given unto many to know the mysteries of God; nevertheless they are laid under a strict command that they shall not impart only according to the portion of his word which he doth grant unto the children of men, according to the heed and diligence which they give unto him.
>
> And therefore, he that will harden his heart, the same receiveth the lesser portion of the word; and he that will not harden his heart, to him is given the greater portion of the word, until it is given unto him to know the mysteries of God until he know them in full.
>
> And *they that will harden their hearts, to them is given the lesser portion of the word until they know nothing concerning his mysteries;* and then they are taken captive by the devil, and led by his will down to destruction. Now this is what is meant by the chains of hell. (Alma 12:9–11, emphasis added)

It might be difficult to understand how a person could lose spiritual knowledge that he once had. But understanding spiritual truths is based on faith and righteousness. Even knowledge gained through our five senses can be lost if there is no faith. Laman and Lemuel *saw* an angel. They *heard* the angel speak unto them. Yet not many years later Laman and Lemuel accuse Nephi of using "cunning arts, that he may deceive our eyes" (1 Nephi 16:38). Somehow they had come to the conclusion that they had neither *seen* nor *heard* an angel, but for a while Nephi had tricked them into believing they had.

George Q. Cannon wrote that a person "professing to be a believer in the truth and connected with the church" cannot stand still. "He must inevitably progress or go backward."[9] We might liken our spiritual progression or regression to walking up a "down" escalator. If we continue to press forward, we can get to the top. However, if we decide to stop for any reason, we will not remain at the point where we stopped, but will backslide. With no effort to progress on our part, we will soon end up at the very bottom, even if at one time we had been very near the top. In the realm of spiritual things we are either progressing or regressing.

Another effect of apostasy is that Satan gains much more power over the individual, even to the point that the person in apostasy, unwittingly or not, joins Satan's forces in fighting against God's kingdom. An individual may decide that he does not need the Church organization and may leave the Church, fully intending to live a Christlike life on his own. But can that person really maintain the Spirit without the sacrament, without the fellowship of the Saints, without performing vicarious work in the temple, and refusing to serve the Lord in Church callings? The Prophet Joseph Smith said:

> Strange as it may appear at first thought, yet it is no less strange than true, that notwithstanding all the professed determination to live godly, apostates after turning from the faith of Christ, unless they have speedily repented, *have sooner or later fallen into the snares of the wicked one, and have been left destitute of the Spirit of God, to manifest their wickedness in the eyes of multitudes. From apostates the faithful have received the severest persecutions.* Judas was rebuked and immediately betrayed his Lord into the hands of His enemies, because Satan entered into him.[10]

Certainly, not everyone who leaves The Church of Jesus Christ of Latter-day Saints becomes antagonistic toward it. But many of the most virulent anti-Mormons are former members of the faith. Elder Harold B. Lee said, "It seems a curious thing that in all dispensations, our worst enemies have been those within—who have betrayed the works of the Lord. . . . We may well expect to find our Judases among those professing membership, but, unfortunately for them, they are laboring under some kind of evil influences or have devious motives."[11] Elder Neal A. Maxwell spoke of this type of individual when he said, "A few leave the

Church who cannot then leave the Church alone."[12] Why is this the case?

Speaking of some of the early apostates who fought against the Church, Isaac Behunnin told the Prophet Joseph Smith, "If I should leave this Church, I would not do as those men have done: I would go to some remote place where Mormonism had never been heard of, settle down, and no one would ever learn that I knew anything about it." Joseph responded:

> Brother Behunnin, you don't know what you would do. No doubt these men once thought as you do. Before you joined this Church you stood on neutral ground. When the gospel was preached good and evil were set before you. You could choose either or neither. There were two opposite masters inviting you to serve them. When you joined this Church you enlisted to serve God. *When you did that you left the neutral ground, and you never can get back on to it. Should you forsake the Master you enlisted to serve, it will be by the instigation of the evil one, and you will follow his dictation and be his servant.*"[13]

Incidentally, on a positive note, Isaac Behunnin remained faithful to the end of his life.

Another common effect of apostasy is the spreading of doubt and undermining of faith as apostates try to influence others to follow their lead and leave the Church. Perhaps their feelings of guilt for leaving the faith are somewhat dampened if they can somehow convince others to deny their beliefs as well. No matter how ridiculous the arguments of the critic or how odd the false doctrine of the self-proclaimed theologian in his attempts to disprove the Church, if they are drawing followers away from the true Church of Jesus Christ, it is a very serious situation. Elder Mark E. Petersen said, "Seeds are sown, seeds of doubt, disbelief, distrust, disrespect. These seeds are watered; they are nurtured, and finally they become fully developed until they produce their evil fruit."[14]

We are talking about eternal consequences of people's souls. Joseph Fielding Smith wrote this insightful statement:

> The Lord said in one of the early revelations before the organization of the Church that the worth of souls is great in the

> sight of God. Then he said if a man should labor all his days and convert but one soul, he should have great joy in the kingdom of our Father, and if he should convert many souls, then much greater would be that joy. Reversing the picture, he who blinds one soul, he who spreads error, he who destroys, through his teachings, divine truth, truth that would lead a man to the kingdom of God and to its fulness, how great shall be his condemnation and his punishment in eternity. For the destruction of a soul is the destruction of the greatest thing that has ever been created.[15]

Yet another effect of apostasy is the loss of desire to repent. Sin affects our spirituality, and apostasy itself is a sin. Sin always precedes and always accompanies apostasy. The mighty change of heart referred to in the scriptures changes an individual's desires from that of the natural, fallen man to that of a new, spiritual creature, born again, with a yearning to follow Christ. The congregation that listened to King Benjamin's sermon felt the Spirit and "they all cried with one voice, saying: Yea, we believe all the words which thou hast spoken unto us; and also, we know of their surety and truth, *because of the Spirit of the Lord Omnipotent, which has wrought a mighty change in us, or in our hearts, that we have no more disposition to do evil, but to do good continually*" (Mosiah 5:2; emphasis added).

Reverting to the old fallen heart through disobedience and rebellion against God causes the individual to lose sight of eternal perspectives. His desires change from seeking God's will to seeking his own will. The more he sins, the more he seeks his own will, and the less the Spirit will influence him. People who start down this path can get to the point where, like Laman and Lemuel, they become "past feeling" (1 Nephi 17:45), and eventually to the position where "it is everlastingly too late, and your destruction is made sure" (Helaman 13:38). It is not that our Father in Heaven would not allow them to repent. They have simply lost all desire to repent and Satan has sealed them his.

In his book *The Peacegiver,* James L. Ferrell writes: "One transgression, one choice away from the Lord, and what happens? The transgressor becomes blinded to his responsibility for sin, and he begins to fall into the captivity of the devil, which are the chains—the chains of sin—

that keep him from feeling the need or desire to return to the Savior."[16] Ferrell concludes that yielding to temptation is how we become subject to the will of Satan.

When an individual transgresses the laws of God, he does not see or understand things as clearly as he did before sinning. Sin causes a loss of truth and light. Consider the story of Adam and Eve in the Garden of Eden. According to Genesis and Moses, as soon as Adam and Eve transgressed the law by partaking of the fruit of the tree of knowledge of good and evil, they attempted to flee and hide from God's presence. This is out of character for our first parents, who loved God and desired to become like Him. The moment transgression took place, they sought to move away from God rather than draw closer to Him. Hence the question, "Adam, where goest thou?" (see Moses 4:15). Adam was essentially asked to stop and evaluate where he was going—toward or away from God. Transgression can point us in the wrong direction and it takes repentance to turn us back around.

With the loss of the Spirit resulting from personal apostasy, a person can lose his desire to repent, his motivation for obedience to God's commandments, and his understanding that he needs Jesus Christ as his Savior. The apostate loses his born again nature or condition.

Who Is at Risk?

We might be tempted to think that apostasy happens only to those who, for one reason or another, become bitter toward the Church or to a few unstable individuals who believe in strange doctrines or follow fundamentalist cults. The reality is that each of us is susceptible to the influence of the adversary that can draw us away from the path leading to exaltation. Do not think that you are immune from personal apostasy. The seeds of apostasy exist within each and every member of The Church of Jesus Christ of Latter-day Saints. We live in a fallen world and are inheritors of a fallen nature. Brigham Young said, "The men and women, who desire to obtain seats in the celestial kingdom, will find that they must battle . . . every day."[17] In fact, many members of the Church, whether they know it or not, have partaken of the spirit of apostasy at some time in their lives because every willful sin or misconduct is a type of rebellion against God.

Personal apostasy can and usually does begin with something very small, like a feeling of superiority or pride, criticism of a bishop, doctrinal confusion, or a nagging doubt that can hamper faith. Likely, many of us have experienced these types of things. But if we are not careful, these little things can become huge issues. There may not be a person in the Church who could honestly and safely say, "I would never leave the Church" or "There is nothing that could cause me to lose my faith in the gospel."

Church history is filled with people who at one time had powerful testimonies of the truthfulness of the restoration of the gospel of Jesus Christ and then fell away from the faith. Some, like Oliver Cowdery and Martin Harris, had witnessed spectacular spiritual manifestations and yet fell away from the Church for a time. Other apostates not only refused to return to the faith, but also became bitter enemies of the Church and tried to destroy it.

An interesting example of someone in authority who lost his faith is Thomas B. Marsh. In the early days of the restoration, Thomas B. Marsh was president of the Quorum of the Twelve. He apostatized while the Prophet Joseph Smith was yet alive and left the company of the Saints an embittered man. In 1857 Marsh came to Utah and asked Brigham Young if he might be allowed to rejoin the Church. Thomas B. Marsh spoke to the Saints gathered at the Bowery on the first Sunday in September. He admitted he had been wrong and promised that if he were permitted to come back into the Church, he would never leave it again.

At the conclusion of the remarks made by Thomas B. Marsh and his plea to the Saints to allow him to reunite with them, President Brigham Young stood and addressed the congregation. He called for a vote to see if the people were willing to welcome Thomas B. Marsh back into full fellowship through rebaptism. With uplifted hands the entire congregation made it known that they were ready to receive Brother Marsh back into the Church.

After the sustaining vote, Brigham Young continued his address to those in attendance at the Bowery that day. He said, "I presume that Brother Marsh will take no offense if I talk a little about him." President Young then proceeded to talk about Marsh's apostasy and his subsequent suffering. He spoke of things that had troubled Thomas B. Marsh and of his weaknesses. Near the conclusion of this address Brigham Young said: "If he [Thomas B. Marsh] had good sense and judgment, he would not have spoken as he has. He has just said, 'I will be faithful, and I will be true to you.' He has not wisdom enough to see that he has betrayed us once, and don't know but what he will again. He has told me that he would be faithful, and that he would do this and the other; but he don't know what he will do next week or next year."[18]

While we may not be impressed with Brigham Young's tactfulness in this situation, we need to recognize the powerful message being given to the Saints by the prophet of God, that no one is completely safe from the influence of evil. President Young concluded his remarks speaking for himself: "I do not know what I shall do next year; . . . You never hear me say that I was going to be true to my God; for I know too much of human weakness; *but I pray God to preserve me from falling away.*"[19]

These are the last days—the final dispensation before the Second Coming of the Lord Jesus Christ. There will not be another Great Apostasy as there was some years after the mortal ministry of Jesus. When the resurrected John the Baptist appeared to Joseph Smith and Oliver Cowdery along the bank of the Susquehanna River in May 1829, not only did he restore the Aaronic Priesthood to the earth, he also promised that this authority would "never be taken again from the earth" (D&C 13:1).

Although there will never again be a general apostasy of the Church, individual apostasy during this last dispensation is more than a possibility—it is a reality. In the April 1969 General Conference, Ezra Taft Benson said:

> One of the grand promises which the Lord made when he restored his Church in these latter days was that the Church should never again be taken from the earth nor given to another people. This

is reassuring, for no matter how much individual apostasy we may see occur among Church members, the Church itself shall endure and remain intact. *Our task, then, is to see that we personally endure to the end in faithful fellowship with the Church.*[20]

In Matthew chapter 13 we find a parable given by the Savior about a wheat field where the enemy had sown tares among the wheat. Tares are noxious weeds that resemble true wheat to such an extent they cannot be distinguished from each other until the grain begins to ripen. Matthew tells us that "the field is the world; the good seed are the children of the kingdom; but the tares are the children of the wicked one" (Matthew 13:38). In a latter-day revelation to the Prophet Joseph Smith, we are given a greater understanding of the symbolic meaning of the parable of the wheat and the tares.

> Behold, verily I say, the field was the world, and the apostles were the sowers of the seed;
>
> And after they have fallen asleep [after the death of the apostles] the great persecutor of the church, the apostate, the whore, even Babylon, that maketh all nations to drink of her cup, in whose hearts the enemy, even Satan, sitteth to reign—behold he soweth the tares; [Satan spreads apostasy] wherefore, the tares choke the wheat and drive the church into the wilderness [the Great Apostasy causes the priesthood to be taken and the true Church of Jesus Christ to be lost from the earth].
>
> But behold, in the last days, even now while the Lord is beginning to bring forth the word, and the blade is springing up and is yet tender [in the latter days when the restoration of the true Church of Jesus Christ has begun]—
>
> Behold, verily I say unto you, the angels are crying unto the Lord day and night, who are ready and waiting to be sent forth to reap down the fields;
>
> But the Lord saith unto them, pluck not up the tares while the blade is yet tender (for verily your faith is weak), lest you destroy the wheat also [after the restoration of the gospel has taken place and the restored Church is growing, clearly there are still going to be tares among the wheat].
>
> Therefore, let the wheat and the tares grow together until the

> harvest is fully ripe; then ye shall first gather out the wheat from among the tares, and after the gathering of the wheat, behold and lo, the tares are bound in bundles, and the field remaineth to be burned. (D&C 86:2–7)

Why does our Father in Heaven not only allow the tares to remain, but commands His angels to leave the tares alone until they are fully ripe? One reason is that the young and tender blades of wheat near the tares might be damaged or destroyed. Elder James E. Talmage explains: "Inspired by zeal for their Master's profit, the servants would have forcibly rooted up the tares, but were restrained, for their unwise though well-intended course would have endangered the wheat while yet tender, since in the early stages of growth it would have been difficult to distinguish the one from the other, and the intertwining of the roots would have caused much destruction of the precious grain."[21]

Another reason for God's patience with the tares is His love for His children who have become tares. His work and His glory are to "bring to pass the immortality and eternal life of man" (Moses 1:39). The Book of Mormon teaches that the Savior, who is like the Father and united with the Father in His efforts, "doeth not anything save it be for the benefit of the world" (2 Nephi 26:24). In nature, wheat is wheat and tares are tares. But this is not true in the analogy of the children of the kingdom and the children of the wicked one. Because of God's great mercy and the Atonement of Jesus Christ, tares can become wheat.

Alma the Younger and the sons of Mosiah were "tares" to the kingdom of God. They were described as the "vilest of sinners" (Mosiah 28:4). Because of the benevolent and forgiving nature of a loving Father and through their faith in the Lord Jesus Christ and sincere repentance, Alma the Younger and the sons of Mosiah became righteous servants of God. They became wheat.

In the eighth chapter of John a woman "taken in adultery" by the scribes and Pharisees was then brought to the Savior to see how He would judge her. This, of course, was a trap set by the scribes and Pharisees to catch Jesus in what they hoped would appear to be an inconsistency in His doctrine. When their plan did not work, and after having their own guilt pointed out to them by Jesus, they departed.

There is an interesting exchange between the Savior and the woman that follows the departure of the scribes and Pharisees. Jesus said to the woman, "Where are those thine accusers? hath no man condemned thee?" The woman replied, "No man, Lord." Then Jesus said, "Neither do I condemn thee; go, and sin no more" (John 8:10–11). Jesus did not say, as some people imagine, "Thy sins are forgiven." She had not believed in Him nor had she repented. She was guilty of adultery. It appears that Jesus was saying, "I do not condemn you now because it is not judgment day. You still have time and opportunity to repent. Go and sin no more." The Joseph Smith Translation of the Bible adds this great conclusion to the incident: "And the woman glorified God from that hour, and believed on his name" (John 8:11, JST).

God loves His children and provides them opportunities for change and growth. We are allowed agency to become what we will be. Tares can become wheat, but also be aware that wheat can become tares. Apostasy is the process of wheat becoming tares, of children of the kingdom becoming children of the wicked one. Again, quoting from the April 1969 General Conference address from Ezra Taft Benson:

> Yes, within the Church today there are tares among the wheat and wolves within the flock. As President Clark stated, "The ravening wolves are amongst us, from our own membership, and they, more than any others, are clothed in sheep's clothing because they wear the habiliments of the priesthood. . . . We should be careful of them. . . ." (*Era,* May 1949, p. 268. See also, *Conference Report,* April 1949, p. 163.)
>
> The wolves amongst our flock are more numerous and devious today than when President Clark made this statement.
>
> President McKay has said that "the Church is little, if at all, injured by persecution and calumnies from ignorant, misinformed or malicious enemies. A greater hindrance to its progress comes from faultfinders, shirkers, commandment-breakers, and apostate cliques within its own ecclesiastical and quorum groups." (*Era,* December 1967, p. 35. See also, *Conference Report,* October 1967, p. 9.)

> Not only are there apostates within our midst, but there are also apostate doctrines that are sometimes taught in our classes and from our pulpits and that appear in our publications. And these apostate precepts of men cause our people to stumble. As the Book of Mormon, speaking of our day, states: ". . . they have all gone astray save it be a few, who are the humble followers of Christ; nevertheless, they are led, that in many instances they do err because they are taught by the precepts of men." (2 Nephi 28:14)[22]

Elder Neal A. Maxwell wrote that wheat and tares are not distinguishable in the early stages. Thus, they will grow side by side until the end comes or until the "wheat becomes more like wheat and the tares become more like tares."[23] This condition of having tares within the wheat or foolish virgins among the wise will exist in the Church until the Second Coming of Christ. Elder Maxwell also said:

> Church members will live in this wheat-and-tares situation until the Millennium. Some real tares even masquerade as wheat, including the few eager individuals who lecture the rest of us about Church doctrines in which they no longer believe. They criticize the use of Church resources to which they no longer contribute. They condescendingly seek to counsel the Brethren whom they no longer sustain. Confrontive, except of themselves, of course, they leave the Church, but they cannot leave the Church alone. Like the throng on the ramparts of the "great and spacious building," they are intensely and busily preoccupied, pointing fingers of scorn at the steadfast iron-rodders (1 Nephi 8:26–28, 33). Considering their ceaseless preoccupation, one wonders, "Is there no diversionary activity available to them, especially in such a large building—like a bowling alley?" Perhaps in their mockings and beneath the stir are repressed doubts of their doubts.[24]

There are situations where the tares manifest themselves in blatant, open apostasy, and Church disciplinary action is taken. Occasionally an apostate is excommunicated from the Church. However, because many "closet apostates" are careful to maintain their membership in the Church, we must not be lulled into thinking that everyone who is a member of the Church is a faithful, loyal believer. Elder Boyd K. Packer shared an experience he had with President Henry D. Moyle:

> We were driving back from Arizona and were talking about a man who destroyed the faith of young people from the vantage point of a teaching position. Someone asked President Moyle why this man was still a member of the Church when he did things like that. "He is not a member of the Church," President Moyle answered firmly. Another replied that he had not heard of his excommunication. "He has excommunicated himself," President Moyle responded. "He has cut himself off from the Spirit of God. Whether or not we get around to holding a court [now known as a disciplinary council] doesn't matter that much; he has cut himself off from the Spirit of the Lord."[25]

Speaking of the dangers that families face in the last days, Elder James E. Faust said, "Among the assaults on families are the attacks on our faith, for which parents should prepare their children. Some of it is coming from apostates who had testimonies and now seem unable to leave the Church alone. . . . The anger and venom of our enemies seems to be increasing."[26]

Apostasy is a very real threat in our day. No one is totally safe from its influence, and when it happens to people you know and care about, it can be devastating. We must prepare and protect our families and ourselves. Awareness of what can lead to apostasy is a vital key to our spiritual safety.

NOTES

1. Steven L. Shields, in *Scattering of the Saints: Schism within Mormonism,* ix.
2. Ibid., vii.
3. Boyd K. Packer, "On Zion's Hill," *Ensign,* Nov. 2005, 73.
4. Oaks, *The Lord's Way,* 247.
5. Gilbert W. Scharffs, "Apostate," in *Encyclopedia of Mormonism,* 1:59.
6. McConkie, *Mormon Doctrine,* 45, emphasis added.
7. Smith, *History of the Church,* 5:340.
8. George Q. Cannon, "What is Apostasy," *Deseret News,* 3 Nov. 1869, 457, emphasis added.
9. George Q. Cannon, "Apostasy and Its Causes," *Deseret News,* 3 Nov. 1869, 457.
10. Smith, *History of the Church,* 2:23, emphasis added.

11. Harold B. Lee, "Make Our Lord and Master Your Friend," *Improvement Era,* Dec. 1968, 71.
12. Neal A. Maxwell, "The Net Gathers of Every Kind," *Ensign,* Nov. 1980, 14.
13. "Recollections of the Prophet Joseph Smith," *Juvenile Instructor,* vol. 28, no. 16, Aug. 15, 1892, 492.
14. Mark E. Peterson, "A Work of Conversion," *Improvement Era,* June 1953, 423.
15. Smith, *Take Heed to Yourselves,* 190.
16. Ferrell, *The Peacegiver,* 160.
17. Brigham Young, in *Journal of Discourses,* 11:14.
18. Brigham Young, in *Journal of Discourses,* 5:212.
19. Ibid., 5:212–13, emphasis added.
20. Ezra Taft Benson, "To the Humble Followers of Christ," *Improvement Era,* June 1969, 42, emphasis added.
21. Talmage, *Jesus the Christ,* 287.
22. Ezra Taft Benson, "To the Humble Follwers of Christ," *Improvement Era,* June 1969, 43.
23. Maxwell, *Deposition of a Disciple,* 63.
24. Neal A. Maxwell, "Becometh As a Child," *Ensign,* May 1996, 68.
25. Packer, *Let Not Your Heart Be Troubled,* 109–110, parenthetical comment added.
26. James E. Faust, "Enriching Family Life," *Ensign,* May 1983, 40.

3

Apostate Groups of the Latter Days and Future Apostasy

Most Latter-day Saints are aware that there are other churches that base their existence and their doctrine, at least in part, on the restoration of the gospel through the Prophet Joseph Smith. Typically, we think of the beginning of these divergent groups taking place after the martyrdom of Joseph and Hyrum Smith. We need to understand that apostate groups began to appear long before the death of the Prophet Joseph. The following are some selected examples of groups and individuals that have apostatized from the Church restored by Joseph Smith.

Apostasy during the Time of Joseph Smith

Some individuals were on the verge of apostasy within a few months of the official formation of the Church. During the late summer of 1830, Hiram Page purported to be receiving revelations for the Church through a seer stone. These revelations were at odds with the revelations Joseph Smith had received. Some people were deceived by Page's revelations, including Oliver Cowdery and several of the Whitmer family. It took some reasoning on the part of Joseph and a revelation from God to squelch this apostate movement (see D&C 28).

Pure Church of Christ (Wycam Clark)

The earliest organized apostate groups appeared during 1831, about a year after Joseph organized the Church. Wycam Clark was baptized about the same time that Sidney Rigdon came into the Church. During the early part of the Kirtland era, Clark, Northrop Sweet, and a few others left the Church. Clark claimed to have received a revelation that he was a prophet. Six men, including Clark and Sweet, organized The Pure Church of Christ. The organization held a few meetings and was disbanded.[1]

John Noah

Another man in Kirtland claiming to be a prophet was John Noah. Ultimately, he was excommunicated. Although there is no record of John Noah starting a church organization, he had at least one disciple who had been a member of the restored Church. The following comes from the journal of Brigham Young:

> A man named Hawley, while plowing his field in the State of New York, had an impression rest down on his mind, with great weight, that he must go to Kirtland and tell Joseph Smith that the Lord had rejected him as a Prophet. He accordingly started right off, with his bare feet, and, on arriving at Kirtland, told Joseph that the Lord had rejected him for allowing John Noah, a Prophet of God, to be cut off from the Church, and for allowing the women to wear caps and the men to wear cushions on their coat sleeves. He was called up before the Bishop's court and disfellowshipped.
>
> He went through the streets of Kirtland one morning, after midnight, and cried, "Woe! Woe! unto the inhabitants of this place." I put my pants and shoes on, took my cow-hide, went out, and laying hold of him, jerked him round, and assured him that if he did not stop his noise and let the people enjoy their sleep without interruption, I would cow-hide him on the spot, for we had the Lord's Prophet right here, and we did not want the Devil's prophet yelling round the streets. The nuisance was forthwith abated.[2]

Church of Christ (Warren Parrish)

Another Kirtland break-off church was begun by Warren Parrish. Parrish had served as a missionary companion to David W. Patten, was a scribe to Joseph Smith, a member of Zion's Camp, and was in the First Quorum of the Seventy in Kirtland. He became part of the large apostate movement that began with the failure of the Kirtland Safety Society, a type of bank begun by Church leaders. However, it is doubtful that the failure of the Kirtland Safety Society was the only reason behind Parrish's apostasy. He served as a clerk and a cashier in the Safety Society, but had embezzled more than twenty-five thousand dollars from the bank, contributing to its demise.[3]

Warren Parrish and three of this dispensation's first apostles, John F. Boynton, Luke S. Johnson, and Lyman E. Johnson, along with several others, left the Church and began their own church. They claimed that it was Joseph Smith who had gone astray from true restoration principles and that they were the old standard. They called their organization the Church of Christ and worked toward the overthrow of the Church that Joseph had established.[4]

From the biography of Lorenzo Snow comes this troubling account about Warren Parrish's group:

> They linked themselves together in an opposing part—pretended that they constituted the Church, and claimed that the temple belonged to them, and even attempted to hold it.
>
> Warren Parrish, who had been a humble, successful preacher of the gospel, was the ringleader of this apostate party. One Sabbath morning, he, with several of his party, came into the temple armed with pistols and bowie-knives and seated themselves together in the Aaronic pulpits, on the east end of the temple, while father Smith and others, as usual, occupied those of the Melchizedek priesthood on the west. Soon after the usual opening services, one of the brethren on the west stand arose, and just after he commenced to speak, one on the east interrupted him. Father Smith, presiding, called to order—he told the apostate brother that he must wait his turn—as the brother on the west took the floor and commenced first to speak, he must not be interrupted. A fearful scene ensued—the apostate speaker becoming so clamorous that Father Smith called for the police to take that man out of the house, when Parrish, John Boynton, and others, drew their pistols and bowie-knives, and rushed down from the stand into the congregation; Boynton saying he would blow out the brains of the first man who dared to lay hands on him. Many in the congregation, especially women and children, were ter-

> ribly frightened—some tried to escape from the confusion by jumping out of the windows. Amid screams and shrieks, the policemen, in ejecting the belligerents, knocked down a stovepipe, which fell helter-skelter among the people; but, although bowie-knives and pistols were wrested from their owners, and thrown hither and thither to prevent disastrous results, no one was hurt, and after a short, but terrible scene to be enacted in a temple of God, order was restored, and the services of the day proceeded as usual.[5]

Warren Parrish's group wrote letters to converts in areas where they had served as missionaries to undermine the Church and the work of the missionaries working there at the time and to other areas where the Church was beginning to grow.[6] Parrish's Church of Christ lasted for only a short time. A number of people who had followed him made their way back to the Church under Joseph Smith's leadership. Heber C. Kimball chanced upon Warren Parrish while crossing the Fox River on a ferry in 1844. Parrish asked Heber C. Kimball to "have the goodness not to say to the people here that I ever was a Mormon. I am a Baptist minister. I am preaching at that meetinghouse for a salary of $500 a year. If they find out I have been a Mormon, it would hurt my influence very much indeed."[7]

Isaac Russell

Isaac Russell was one of the missionaries that accompanied Heber C. Kimball on the first British mission for the Church. He was with Elder Kimball, Willard Richards, and Orson Hyde when they experienced a terrifying confrontation with forces of the adversary on July 30, 1837, in Preston, England.[8]

After returning from his mission in England, Isaac Russell and his family settled in Missouri, where they were persecuted with the other Mormons in Missouri at that time. The reason for Russell's apostasy appears to have been based on the revelation given through Joseph Smith that the Twelve would leave on their missions on April 26, 1839, from the temple site in Far West, Missouri. After the Saints had been driven from Missouri, Russell did not believe that this revelation could be fulfilled.

A number of the Twelve did return to Far West, Missouri, arriving shortly after midnight on April 26 and in the hours before dawn held a meeting. One item of business at that meeting was the excommunication of a number of dissidents, including Isaac Russell.[9]

Theodore Turley was attending that meeting with the Twelve in Far West, Missouri. As they were leaving the area that morning, Turley requested the company to stop while he bid farewell to his friend, Isaac Russell. Russell's wife answered the door and called to her husband, "It is brother Turley." Russell was surprised because Turley and the rest of the Saints had departed that area two weeks earlier and Russell believed it to be too dangerous for any of the Mormons to return.

Discovering that it indeed was Theodore Turley, Russell invited him to sit down, to which Turley replied, "I cannot; I shall lose my company." When Russell asked who Turley's company was, he was answered, "The Twelve, . . . don't you know that this is the twenty-sixth, and the day the Twelve were to take leave of their friends on the foundation of the Lord's House, to go to the islands of the sea? The revelation is now fulfilled, and I am going with them."[10]

Isaac Russell had lost faith in Joseph Smith and his role as prophet of God. Russell eventually came to believe that, instead of Joseph Smith, he was to lead the Saints into the wilderness, where he would be given instructions to minister to the Lamanites. He also taught that the Three Nephites would be sent to his group to assist them in building up Zion. About twenty Latter-day Saints chose to follow Isaac Russell.[11]

Russell wrote a letter to Latter-day Saint converts in Alton, England, dated January 30, 1839. The following are excerpts from that letter:

> I charge you to read this letter to none but those who enter into a covenant with you to keep those things that are revealed in this letter from all the world, and from all churches, except the churches to whom I myself have ministered. . . .
>
> The Lamanites, who are spoken of in the Book of Mormon, have all been driven to the western boundaries of the States of America, by the Gentiles, as I told you; they have now to be visited by the

> gospel, for the day of their redemption is come, and the Gentiles have now well nigh filled up the measure of their wickedness, and will soon be cut off. . . .
>
> Now the thing that I have to reveal to you is sacred, and must be kept with care; for I am not suffered to reveal it at all to the churches in this land, because of their wickedness and unbelief—for they have almost cast me out from amongst them, because I have testified of their sins to them, and warned them of the judgments that have yet to come upon them; and this thing that I now tell you, will not come to the knowledge of the churches until they are purified.
>
> Now the thing is as follows—The Lord has directed me, with a few others, whose hearts the Lord has touched, to go into the wilderness, where we shall be fed and directed by the hand of the Lord until we are purified and prepared to minister to the Lamanites, and with us the Lord will send those three who are spoken of in the Book of Mormon, who were with Jesus after His resurrection, and have tarried on the earth to minister to their brethren in the last days. . . .
>
> We have not yet gone into the wilderness, but we shall go when the Lord appoints the time. If you should hear that I have apostatized, believe it not, for I am doing the work of the Lord.[12]

Isaac Russell's new church was not very successful. When his own religious movement faltered, Russell did not reunite with the Church but remained in Missouri until his death in 1844.

Oliver Olney

Oliver Olney joined the Church during the Kirtland era. He eventually ended up in Nauvoo. Several articles from the Nauvoo newspaper *Times and Seasons* give us a glimpse of his apostasy from the Church. One article stated that "Mr. Olney has long been a member of this church, and until within two or three years ago, has always maintained a consistent character."[13]

Evidently, Olney claimed that he had seen and conversed with Adam, the ancient of days, and that he had received many revelations. Although he told people that he was receiving revelations, when questioned by Church leaders he refused to bring the revelations forward or have them examined. Olney was tried by the Nauvoo High Council and disfellowshipped "because he would not have his writings tested by the word of God; evidently proving that he loves darkness rather than light, because his deeds are evil."[14] It was also reported that after he became "wild and visionary" and "loosed from the moorings of eternal truth" Olney was duped into believing the word of apostate John C. Bennett.[15]

Olney published two pamphlets, *The Absurdities of Mormonism Portrayed* in 1843 and *Spiritual Wifery at Nauvoo Exposed* in 1845.[16] The name of Oliver Olney later appeared in a letter written by Wilford Woodruff from England. Elder Woodruff reported that the *London Times* had quoted certain revelations by Olney that had been published in the United States.[17] It is not known whether he began an organized church and had followers. Nothing else is known about Oliver Olney after he left the Church.

Apostasy following the Death of the Prophet Joseph

At the death of Joseph and Hyrum Smith it was not clear to many of the Saints how the Church would proceed and whom the Saints should follow.[18] Claims for being the legitimate successor to Joseph Smith came not only from the Twelve but also from Sidney Rigdon, Alpheus Cutler, James J. Strang, and many others. Although the majority of the Saints followed Brigham Young and the Twelve, others made their way into alternative church organizations. A number of these churches only lasted a short time, while others exist to this day. I will briefly mention a few of these groups below.

Church of Christ (Sidney Rigdon)

Sidney Rigdon was a Baptist minister and a Campbellite preacher before joining the Church in November 1830. After meeting Joseph Smith the following month, the two were almost constantly together for years. Rigdon was known for his powerful preaching and became one of the most influential people in the early Church. He was sustained as first counselor to Joseph Smith in the Presidency of the Church in March 1833.

Rigdon helped Joseph with the new translation of the Bible and gave a powerful sermon at the dedication of the Kirtland Temple. He also co-witnessed the vision with Joseph Smith now known as section 76 of the Doctrine and Covenants, and suffered many persecutions with the Saints, including being imprisoned with the Prophet Joseph in Liberty Jail.

After the Saints settled in Nauvoo, Sidney Rigdon did not play as major a role in Church leadership as he previously had. Although part of this was due to illness, it also appears that Joseph had lost some confidence in Rigdon. In 1843 Joseph tried to have Sidney Rigdon released from his position as counselor in the First Presidency, but Hyrum Smith and others persuaded Joseph to give Rigdon another chance. Joseph is reported to have said, "I have thrown him off my shoulders, and you have again put him on me."[19]

Of Rigdon during the Nauvoo period historian Glen M. Leonard wrote:

> Even though Sidney Rigdon still held the position of first counselor at the time of the martyrdom, he had moved his family to his native Pittsburg to reestablish residence as the vice-presidential candidate on Joseph Smith's union ticket. . . . The Prophet's able spokesman had been a reluctant resident of Nauvoo, anxious since 1841 to seek a place of refuge away from the appointed stake, even though enjoined by the Prophet not to do so. Rigdon had declared his unwillingness to follow the Prophet's revelations if they inconvenienced him personally.[20]

Upon hearing the news of Joseph's death, Rigdon rushed back to Nauvoo, arriving before many of the Quorum of the Twelve had returned. He wanted to hold a meeting before the rest of the Twelve returned, claiming that no one could replace Joseph Smith, but that he [Rigdon] should lead the Church as its "guardian." The meeting to decide succession was postponed until Brigham Young and others of the Twelve returned to Nauvoo.

On August 8, 1844, a meeting was held to determine who would lead the Church. Sidney Rigdon spoke in the morning, offering his services as guardian of the Church. In the afternoon Brigham Young and

Amasa Lyman spoke on behalf of the Twelve leading the Church. The decision was put to a vote of the congregation, which overwhelmingly sustained Brigham Young and the Twelve.[21]

Rigdon was bitter and soon began attempts to undermine the authority of the Twelve. He was excommunicated and returned to Pittsburg. In October 1844 he established his own newspaper called the *Latter Day Saints' Messenger and Advocate,* in which he attacked the Church and its leaders. In their periodical Rigdon and his followers claimed that Joseph Smith had become a fallen prophet and had been "cut off by the Lord" in the early 1840s.[22]

On April 6, 1844, Rigdon founded the Church of Christ, of which he was president. His church organization included a Quorum of Twelve Apostles, seventies, a high council, a bishopric, and a stake presidency over a stake established in Pittsburg. The exact number of members of Rigdon's church is not known, but it was reported to have been sizeable.[23]

The year 1845 appears to have been the high point of Rigdon's Church of Christ. Members began to fall away in 1846 and by 1847 there were just a few loyal believers that remained. In 1869 Rigdon attempted to reunite his few scattered followers into another church organization, but the attempt failed. In 1863 Brigham Young invited Sidney Rigdon to move to Utah, but Rigdon rejected his invitation.[24]

Church of Jesus Christ (Alpheus Cutler)

Alpheus Cutler joined the Church in January 1833. He became a prominent member of the Church, serving on the Nauvoo Stake High Council. He left Nauvoo with a company of Saints in 1847 and settled for a few years in Kanesville, Iowa.

As most of the Saints went west to the Great Basin, Cutler remained in Iowa as leader of a group of settlers who created a community they named Manti. Cutler claimed that while Joseph Smith was yet alive, he had revealed to Cutler that "a sign of two half moons with their backs together would be seen by him [Cutler] when the proper time to reorganize the church had arrived."[25] According to his biography, Cutler did see the sign of the two half moons during 1853.[26] Consequently,

Alpheus Cutler organized the Church of Jesus Christ on September 19, 1853, at Manti, Iowa.

The entire settlement of Manti, about thirty families, became part of the Church of Jesus Christ. Each member was required to be rebaptized because, as Cutler saw it, his church was not a continuation of the church begun by Joseph Smith, but a reorganization of that church. This reorganization became necessary because Cutler believed that Joseph's church had been rejected by God when Brigham Young took control.[27]

Alpheus Cutler passed away on August 10, 1864, and Chauncey Whiting replaced Cutler as leader of the church. The group later relocated to western Minnesota. By the late 1920s the active membership of the Cutler faction had dwindled to about thirty people.[28]

Some of the Church of Jesus Christ membership moved to Independence, Missouri, beginning in 1928 with the Fletcher family. Today, the church has a small white meetinghouse just a few blocks from the Community of Christ temple and the LDS stake center and visitors' center. In 1993 I spoke to a member of the Fletcher family who lived next to the church and was told at that time there were about twenty-five members of their faith. I understand that there are now fewer than twenty remaining active members of the church begun by Alpheus Cutler.[29]

Church of Christ—Temple Lot (Granville Hedrick)

At the time of Joseph's and Hyrum's death in Carthage, Illinois, there were several existing branches of the Church in central Illinois and one in Indiana. Rather than follow Brigham Young and the Twelve or any of the other factions, these branches eventually merged into one organization they called the Church of Christ.

Granville Hedrick had been an elder in the original Church founded by Joseph Smith. After the Prophet's death, Hedrick moved from one faction to another until he and others formed the Church of Christ. Although Hedrick was only one of the founders, he became the church's first president.

Hedrick claimed that he received a revelation in 1863 instructing his church members to return to Missouri and reclaim Zion. Nearly sixty of Hedrick's group began the trek to Missouri during the winter of 1866–67. They not only returned to Independence, Missouri, but they were also able to obtain the lot that had been designated by Joseph Smith for the building of the temple.

When the Reorganized Church (now known as the Community of Christ) moved back to Independence, they found Hedrick's group already there with ownership of the temple lot. The RLDS Church took the Church of Christ to court to obtain the temple lot. Their case was unsuccessful, and the Hedrick group maintained possession, which they have to this day. For this reason they are typically known as the Church of Christ (Temple Lot).

The Church of Christ reached their peak in membership about 1930 with approximately four thousand members. Membership declined after that time, primarily because of schisms within the group: one faction became known as the Fettingites, with another faction commonly called Draveites.

The headquarters of the Church of Christ is Independence, Missouri, on a lot adjacent to the temple lot. Depending on the source, current membership is estimated to be somewhere between two and three thousand.[30]

Community of Christ (Formerly Known as the Reorganized Church of Jesus Christ of Latter Day Saints)

Jason W. Briggs joined The Church of Jesus Christ of Latter-day Saints in 1841. Following the death of Joseph Smith, Briggs first stayed with the majority of the Saints who followed Brigham Young and the Twelve. As the Saints moved west, Briggs left the Church and united with the schism started by James J. Strang. Following his time in Strang's church, for a short period Briggs became part of William Smith's group.

Briggs declared that his concern about who held the true authority led him to seek divine guidance. He said that the answer, which came to him in November 1851, was that it would be a descendant of Joseph Smith who rightly should preside over the restored church.

Several months later a copy of Briggs's revelation was delivered to Zenos Gurley, Sr., who attested to having received a confirmation that the revelation was true. The message was spread to several existing branches of Latter-day Saints who had not gone west with Brigham Young. A conference of these congregations met in the summer of 1852 to consider Brigg's revelation. Of this conference, Community of Christ historian, Roger D. Launius wrote:

> It had no acknowledged head, no organization for which to transact business, no authority to act, and no business to transact. It was united only in its opposition to other Mormon factions, in its acceptance of the Briggs document as divine revelation, in its belief that Mormonism as set forth in the Scriptures was correct, and in its affirmation that the proper successor to the prophetic office was growing to maturity in Nauvoo and would one day step forth to accept his calling.[31]

Eventually, this New Organization of the Church of Jesus Christ of Latter Day Saints selected apostles, including Briggs and Gurley, with Briggs as the presiding officer. In the years that followed, efforts were made by members of the New Organization to persuade Joseph Smith III to accept the role as leader of their church. For several years young Joseph did not respond to anything communicated to him from their church.

In 1856 Briggs and Gurley traveled to Nauvoo to speak in person with Joseph III. He told them that he was not interested in their proposal that he become involved with the Reorganization. However, after several years of financial setbacks, which he later saw as humbling preparation experiences, Joseph Smith III agreed to take the leadership of the church begun by Briggs and Gurley.

At a conference in Amboy, Illinois, held on April 6, 1860, Joseph Smith III was accepted and ordained as President of the Reorganized Church of Jesus Christ of Latter Day Saints. He held that position for over fifty years until his death in November 1914.

Except for The Church of Jesus Christ of Latter-day Saints, the Reorganized Church has been the largest organization that bases its beliefs on the gospel restoration through Joseph Smith.[32] There have been substantial changes in recent years, including the 1984 pronouncement allowing women in their church to hold the priesthood, the 1996 decision that it was no longer necessary that the church be led by a descendant of Joseph Smith, and the April 2000 changing of the name of the church to the Community of Christ.[33]

The changes made within the Community of Christ have resulted in some dissent. Many former members of the church have created the restoration branches movement, "some claiming outright rejection of the reorganization, others seeking to remain a part of the organization and attempting to change it from within."[34]

Break-off Groups Continue to Appear

The Prophet Joseph Smith restored God's true church to the earth. As we have seen, since that time those who have rejected Joseph as a prophet or who have wandered from the priesthood path that Joseph established have committed acts of apostasy. Some have rejected the gospel to such an extent that they have become apostates and enemies to God's kingdom. As shown earlier in this chapter, apostasy from the Church began during Joseph's life and became more widespread after his death; and apostasy continues to happen to this day.

A number of years ago I began researching groups that broke away from The Church of Jesus Christ of Latter-day Saints or those who base their doctrine, at least in part, on the restoration of the gospel through the Prophet Joseph Smith. This would include the break-offs from the break-offs, of which there are many. At that time I could account for about one hundred seventy-five groups that would qualify since the Restoration in 1830. Of the one hundred seventy-five, somewhere between fifty and seventy were still in existence.

In recent years there have been numerous additions to these splinter groups. They seem to appear and sometimes disappear almost overnight. One researcher reports that there have now been at least four hundred groups that sprang from the restoration movement of Joseph Smith.[35] I heard recently that one author who is chronicling these different groups is challenged with new groups appearing so frequently that he has to simply come up with a cut-off date to stop counting so he can finish his book.

Most of these break-off groups are not very large, and the majority of their members have never been affiliated with The Church of Jesus Christ of Latter-day Saints. We might consider them to be misguided, but could not really regard them as apostates. They are predominantly good people who are doing what they believe is right. There are, however, a few apostate groups that can be considered harmful and dangerous—from Internet chat rooms that have broken up marriages to child abuse and even murder.[36]

Even the most harmless and unassuming of these groups can still be damaging to those who are looking for the gospel fulness. The majority of their followers may be sincere, but the organizations themselves were born of apostasy. They testify of the Book of Mormon and of the Prophet Joseph Smith, and many of their other doctrines are true. The imitation is often so close to the real thing that, figuratively speaking, the devil truly has appeared as an angel of light.

Apostasy to Continue

This is the dispensation of the fulness of times, the last dispensation before the second coming of Jesus Christ. We have been promised that there will not be another great apostasy. We know that the gospel of Jesus Christ will never be taken again from the earth. But we also know that some will fall away from the truth. Some will wander from the correct path onto strange roads because they are deceived. Others will follow forbidden paths through rebellion and pride. But make no mistake, individual apostasy from the Church will continue to take place until the Millennium is ushered in by Christ's return.

Apostasy After the Millennium

As Latter-day Saints we view the coming millennial reign of Jesus Christ on the earth as a time of great joy and peace. The earth will have been cleansed by fire, and the wicked and all evil influences will have been destroyed. "The earth will be renewed and receive its paradisiacal glory," or, in other words, the earth will be raised to the terrestrial condition in which it existed prior to the fall of Adam (Articles of Faith 1:10). Satan will be bound during that time and righteousness will abound. It will be a wonderful time to live.

What we sometimes forget is that there is what the scriptures describe as a "little season" after the Millennium where Satan is loosed and apostasy again appears on the earth. In the allegory of the olive tree recorded in Jacob 5, the prophet Zenos writes of that post-millennial period as the time when evil fruit again comes into the vineyard (Jacob 5:77).

Joseph Smith received this revelation in September 1830: "And again, verily, verily, I say unto you that when the thousand years are ended, and men again begin to deny their God, then will I spare the earth but for a little season" (D&C 29:22). Both righteous and unrighteous will dwell on the earth during this time.

What will happen as this new influx of evil and rebellion emerges into a paradisiacal-level earth? Joseph Fielding Smith explained: "Will the earth go back to the telestial order after the millennium? No, but the people on the face of the earth, many of them, will be like the Nephites who lived 200 years after the coming of Christ. They will rebel against the Lord knowingly, and the great last struggle will come, and the devil and his forces will be defeated; then the earth will die and receive its resurrection and become a celestial body."[37]

At the end of this little season is the time when the final great battle of good versus evil on the earth takes place. "And the devil shall gather together his armies; even the hosts of hell, and shall come up to battle against Michael and his armies. And then cometh the battle of the great God; and the devil and his armies shall be cast away into their own place, that they shall not have power over the saints any more at all" (D&C 88:113–14).

At this point the earth "dies" and is resurrected to a celestial glory. Those worthy of that glory will inherit what had been the earth, but is now a celestial kingdom. Those who enter a celestial glory are "received into the kingdom of the Father to go no more out, but to dwell with God eternally in the heavens" (3 Nephi 28:40). They have become like God, and because they have been tried and tested and found worthy, there will never be any apostasy from among them—they will go no more out.

NOTES

1. George A. Smith, in *Journal of Discourses,* 11:4.
2. Watson, *Manuscript History of Brigham Young 1801–1844,* 17–18. (Spelling and punctuation unchanged.)
3. Roberts, *Comprehensive History of the Church,* 1:405.
4. *Elders' Journal,* July 1838, 37. Later, the three apostles who had been disfellowshipped admitted their error and desired to repent and come back into the Church. They were received back into fellowship and into their places in the Quorum of the Twelve. See Smith, *History of the Church,* 2:528.
5. Smith, *Biography and Family Record of Lorenzo Snow,* 20–21.
6. *Wilford Woodruff's Journal,* vol. 1, 240–41, 412.
7. George A. Smith, in *Journal of Discourses,* 7:115.
8. Whitney, *Life of Heber C. Kimball,* 129–32.
9. Smith, *Church History and Modern Revelation,* 4:17.
10. Watson, *Manuscript History of Brigham Young 1801–1844,* 38–39.
11. George A. Smith, in *Journal of Discourses,* 7:115–16.
12. Smith, *History of the Church,* 3:343–44. (Spelling and punctuation unchanged).
13. *Times and Seasons,* vol. 4, no. 6, February 1, 1843, 89.
14. Ibid.
15. Ibid.
16. Shields, *Divergent Paths of the Restoration,* 27–28.
17. *Times and Seasons,* vol. 6, no. 24, February 15, 1846, 1129.
18. An informative study on the various possibilities for succession is D. Michael Quinn, "The Mormon Succession Crisis of 1844," *BYU Studies,* vol. 16, no. 2, Winter 1976, 187–233.
19. Smith, *History of the Church,* 6:49.
20. Leonard, *Nauvoo: A Place of Peace, A People of Promise,* 429.
21. Roberts, *Comprehensive History of the Church,* 2:414–20.
22. *Latter Day Saints' Messenger and Advocate,* as cited in Quinn, "The Mormon Succession Crisis of 1844," 191.
23. Shields, *Divergent Paths of the Restoration,* 36–38.
24. Rich, *Those Who Would Be Leaders,* 19–20.
25. Fletcher, *Alpheus Cutler and the Church of Jesus Christ,* 47. The authors belonged to Cutler's church. The quote from the book reads "two crescent moons," but the word *crescent* has been crossed out and replaced by the handwritten word *half,* likely written by one of the authors. I purchased the book from their daughter.
26. Ibid.

27. Shields, *Divergent Paths of the Restoration*, 60–61; Rich, *Those Who Would Be Leaders*, 49–51.
28. Danny L. Jorgensen, "Back to Zion: The Emergence of the Church of Jesus Christ (Cutlerite) and Its Return to Independence, Missouri," in Bringhurst and Hamer, *Scattering of the Saints: Schism within Mormonism*, 169.
29. I heard Stephen L. Shields refer to the remaining seventeen members of the church organized by Alpheus Cutler at a conference held at Utah Valley State College in April 2008. In May 2008 my wife and I attended a meeting with the Church of Jesus Christ (Cutlerite) in Independence, Missouri. Leaders of their church told us that they had seventeen active members, with dozens of inactive members of their church. The active members appear to be mainly older people, primarily from two remaining families. They are very warm and friendly people, loyal to the Prophet Joseph Smith and with a firm belief in the Book of Mormon.
30. Information on the Church of Christ (Temple Lot) was obtained from the following sources: Flint, *An Outline History of the Church of Christ (Temple Lot)*; Rich, *Those Who Would Be Leader*, 46–49; Shields, *Divergent Paths of the Restoration*, 76–85; and R. Jean Addams, "The Church of Christ (Temple Lot), Its Emergence, Struggles and Early Schisms," in Bringhurst and Hamer, *Scattering of the Saints: Schism within Mormonism*, 206–23.
31. Launius, *Joseph Smith III: Pragmatic Prophet*, 88.
32. A Community of Christ leader replied to a query made by BYU professor Alonzo Gaskill as to how many members their organization had in 2006. He said that he did not know anyone who could provide a firm number, but he thought they had about 200,000 on the rolls. A film in a Community of Christ visitors' center claims a membership of about 250,000.
33. Information on the Community of Christ was obtained from the following sources: Brighurst and Hamer, eds., *Scattering of the Saints: Schism within Mormonism*; Edwards, *Our Legacy of Faith*; Launius, *Joseph Smith III: Pragmatic Prophet*; Launius and Spillman, eds., *Let Contention Cease*; Shields, *Divergent Paths of the Restoration*; Smith, *Origin of the Reorganized Church*.
34. Steven L. Shields, "An Overview of Dissent in the Reorganization," in Launius and Spillman, eds., *Let Contention Cease*, 77.
35. Steven L. Shields, in Bringhurst and Hamer, *Scattering of the Saints: Schism within Mormonism*, ix.
36. I am familiar with several situations where married LDS women got involved in chat rooms on the Internet with men from break-offs of the Church. In two cases of which I am personally aware, the women abandoned their husbands and young families, moved to Utah, and became plural wives of men

they met online. Also, there have been a number of incidents where members of cults that broke away from the LDS Church killed members from rival groups and, in a few cases, innocent victims unrelated to the radical religious organizations were murdered.

37. Smith, *Doctrines of Salvation,* 1:87.

4

Things That Can Lead to Apostasy

If a study could be done of each apostate since the restoration of the gospel and a list compiled of the reasons each apostasy occurred, it would be lengthy because there are so many underlying causes of apostasy. The most common motives appear to be serious sins without efforts to repent; criticism of Church leaders or faultfinding; a desire for wealth, power, and fame; trying to "steady the ark"; hurt feelings, discontent, or dissatisfaction; tribulations and persecutions; receiving or following false revelations; neglect of duty; and not being willing to change when Church policies are altered or when new revelation comes to the Church through the prophet. Again, this list is in no way comprehensive, but represents the most common reasons for apostasy. Chapters that follow will look in detail at a number of these most frequent causes of apostasy.

Pride is the overriding problem that appears to cause all of the other reasons for apostasy. From the book *Follow the Living Prophets* comes this truism: "No matter what shape apostasy takes, from seemingly harmless murmuring to openly hateful rebellion, it always stems from some sort of pride and always ends in some kind of pain."[1]

Consider the well-known cases of early Church leaders, Oliver Cowdery, Martin Harris, David Whitmer, Sidney Rigdon, and Thomas B. Marsh. Each man left the Church, at least for a time, and pride was the main stumbling block to each of these brethren. How about

Symonds Ryder[2], who left the Church because his name was misspelled by a scribe who recorded a revelation received by Joseph Smith? Can you spell *pride?*

President Ezra Taft Benson's classic discourse on pride contains these insightful statements:

> Pride is a sin that can readily be seen in others but is rarely admitted in ourselves. Most of us consider pride to be a sin of those on the top, such as the rich and the learned, looking down at the rest of us. . . . There is, however, a far more common ailment among us—and that is pride from the bottom looking up. It is manifest in so many ways, such as faultfinding, gossiping, backbiting, murmuring, living beyond our means, envying, coveting, withholding gratitude and praise that might lift another, and being unforgiving and jealous.
>
> Disobedience is essentially a prideful power struggle against someone in authority over us. It can be a parent, a priesthood leader, a teacher, or ultimately God. A proud person hates the fact that someone is above him. He thinks this lowers his position.
>
> Selfishness is one of the more common faces of pride. "How everything affects me" is the center of all that matters—self-conceit, self-pity, worldly self-fulfillment, self-gratification, and self-seeking.
>
> Pride results in secret combinations which are built up to get power, gain, and glory of the world. . . . Pride is the universal sin, the great vice. . . . Pride is the great stumbling block to Zion. I repeat: Pride *is* the great stumbling block to Zion.[3]

President Joseph F. Smith wrote about those members of The Church of Jesus Christ of Latter-day Saints who preach false doctrine disguised as gospel truths. He said that this might be expected almost exclusively from two particular classes of individuals:

> First—The hopelessly ignorant, whose lack of intelligence is due to their indolence and sloth, who make but feeble effort, if indeed any at all, to better themselves by reading and study; those who are afflicted with a dread disease that may develop into an incurable malady—laziness.
>
> Second—*The proud and self-vaunting ones, who read by the lamp of*

> *their own conceit;* who interpret by rules of their own contriving; who have become a law unto themselves, and so pose as the sole judges of their own doings. More dangerously ignorant than the first.[4]

In Luke chapter fifteen a group of publicans and sinners draw close to listen to the Savior teach. The Pharisees and scribes who were nearby murmured to each other about the type of people Jesus would teach and that He would even "eateth with them" (Luke 15:1–2). Knowing what they were talking about, Jesus spoke a parable to the murmuring Pharisees and scribes in the form of a question.

> What man of you, having an hundred sheep, if he lose one of them, doth not leave the ninety and nine in the wilderness, and go after that which is lost, until he find it?
>
> And when he hath found it, he layeth it on his shoulders, rejoicing.
>
> And when he cometh home, he calleth together his friends and neighbours, saying unto them, Rejoice with me; for I have found my sheep which was lost.
>
> I say unto you, that likewise joy shall be in heaven over one sinner that repenteth, more than over ninety and nine just persons, which need no repentance. (Luke 15:4–7)

These verses have often been used to illustrate the worth of a soul and how important it is to reach out to the one who is lost. I have heard it used in this manner: The teacher of the Beehive class has ten girls on the class roll and nine attending regularly. Even though nine out of ten is a very good percentage of those attending, the teacher should go after the one who is lost and bring her to the safety of the fold.

This is a correct *application* of the parable. The worth of each spirit child of our Father in Heaven is great, and we should do all we possibly can to save each and every person. However, the *interpretation* of these verses is quite different. Consider part of verse 7: "Joy shall be in heaven over one sinner that repenteth, more than over ninety and nine just persons, which need no repentance." This particular verse used to trouble me. I recognize what a joyful thing it is for a sinner to repent and return to the path leading to eternal happiness. But can there really be more joy in heaven over one repenting sinner than there is for ninety-nine righteous people who never strayed, but stayed on the path?

The Prophet Joseph Smith said, "I have a key by which I understand the scriptures. I enquire, what was the question which drew out the answer or caused Jesus to utter the parable?"[5] In this case the circumstance that caused Jesus to speak the parable of the lost sheep was the disdain the scribes and Pharisees felt for the publicans and sinners—a disdain born of arrogance and pride. We look to Joseph Smith for the interpretation of this parable: "The hundred sheep represent one hundred Sadducees and Pharisees, as though Jesus had said, 'If you Sadducees and Pharisees are in the sheepfold, I have no mission for you; I am sent to look up sheep that are lost; and when I have found them, I will back them up and make joy in heaven.' This represents hunting after a few individuals, or one poor publican, which the Pharisees and Sadducees despised."[6]

There are two groups of people in these verses: 1) those who know they are sinners and accept Jesus as their Savior because he offers them forgiveness and provides the way back; and 2) those that see themselves as righteous and believe they do not need Jesus to be saved. The second group see themselves as "in the fold" with no need of a Savior because they do not see themselves as lost or needing to be saved. Luke 15:7 says that there is more joy over one repentant sinner than over ninety-nine "just persons, which need no repentance." Who honestly needs *no* repentance? There has only been one perfect person—the Lord Jesus Christ. So who are these people who need no repentance? They are the proud, self-righteous people who *think* they do not need to repent.

People who are prideful have a difficult time repenting because they cannot see themselves as being wrong. President Ezra Taft Benson said: "The proud cannot accept the authority of God giving direction to their lives. They pit their perceptions of truth against God's great knowledge, their abilities versus God's priesthood power, their accomplishments against His mighty works."[7] As President Benson describes it, the central feature of pride is enmity, meaning hatred, hostility, or being in a state of opposition. In the case of the apostate, he has developed an enmity for Church members or Church leaders or even God. "Our enmity toward God takes on many labels, such as rebellion, hard-heartedness, stiff-neckedness, unrepentant, puffed up, easily offended, and sign seekers. The proud wish God would agree with them. They aren't interested in changing their opinions to agree with God's."[8]

We might see a person struggling with Church authority or doctrine and easily recognize the pride in that person's life. Because of our fallen mortal nature, it is not as easy to see pride within ourselves. This makes the possibility of falling into apostasy that much easier because people are often not only blinded to their pride, but blinded by their pride. I have heard it said that the righteous do everything they think is right, while the self-righteous think everything they do is right. To a person blinded by pride "the world shouts louder than the whisperings of the Holy Ghost. The reasoning of men overrides the revelations of God, and the proud let go of the iron rod."[9]

In the Book of Mormon there were secret combinations of apostates that caused the destruction of two civilizations, the Jaredites and the Nephites. President Benson said that it was pride that resulted in these secret combinations. He said that "this fruit of the sin pride, namely secret combinations, . . . will yet be the cause of the fall of many nations."[10] In this last dispensation pride has resulted in the apostasy of a number of people and will yet lead to the apostasy of more members of The Church of Jesus Christ of Latter-day Saints.

Pride sometimes manifests itself in what might be called worldliness. Lorenzo Snow taught that worldliness impedes spiritual progress.[11] Lusting after the things of the world is more than simply wanting wealth and the things that money can buy. Worldliness revels in having more or nicer things than others. C. S. Lewis wrote that "pride gets no pleasure out of having something, only out of having more of it than the next man."[12]

Lewis was particularly attuned to the wickedness of pride. Consider several other comments he made about this evil:

> We say that people are proud of being rich, or clever, or good-looking, but they are not. They are proud of being richer, cleverer, or

better looking than others. If every one else became equally rich, or clever, or good-looking there would be nothing to be proud about. It is the comparison that makes you proud: the pleasure of being above the rest.[13]

It is pride which has been the chief cause of misery in every nation and every family since the world began. . . . Pride always means enmity—it is enmity. And not only enmity between man and man, but enmity to God.[14]

As long as you are proud you cannot know God. A proud man is always looking down on things and people: and, of course, as long as you are looking down, you cannot see something that is above you.[15]

C. S. Lewis understood that pride "is the complete anti-God state of mind."[16] Apostates may give many reasons why they reject the fulness of the gospel of Jesus Christ, but ultimately the reason is pride. Whether it manifests itself in willful rebellion against God and His commandments, criticism of Church leaders, worldliness and greed, or the desire for power and recognition, it is pride that causes us to cut ourselves off from the presence of God.

NOTES

1. Top, Dahl, and Bowen, *Follow the Living Prophets,* 185.
2. Ryder's name is found in Church history as Simonds Ryder, Simonds Rider, Symonds Rider, and the way his signature reads and what is found on his tombstone: Symonds Ryder. See *Doctrines for Exaltation: The 1989 Sperry Symposium on the Doctrine and Covenants,* 271, note 1. I assume the version that is found on his tombstone and his signature is the correct spelling. But who can be completely certain anymore?
3. Ezra Taft Benson, "Beware of Pride," *Ensign,* May 1989, 5–6.
4. Smith, *Gospel Doctrine,* 373, emphasis added.
5. Smith, *Teachings of the Prophet Joseph Smith,* 276–77.
6. Ibid., 277.
7. Ezra Taft Benson, "Beware of Pride," *Ensign,* May 1989, 4.
8. Ibid.
9. Ibid., 5.
10. Ibid., 6.
11. See Snow, *Teachings of Lorenzo Snow,* 130–131.

12. Lewis, *Mere Christianity,* 109.
13. Ibid., 109–110.
14. Ibid., 110–11.
15. Ibid., 111.
16. Ibid., 109.

5

Serious Transgression without Efforts to Repent

Joseph Fielding Smith wrote, "Almost without exception when a person leaves the Church, it is due to transgression. The Spirit of the Lord will not dwell in unclean tabernacles, and when the Spirit is withdrawn, darkness supersedes the light, and apostasy will follow."[1]

Disobedience leads people away from the Lord and from salvation. Sin numbs the spiritual senses and weakens moral strength. The more serious a person's transgressions, the more difficult it becomes for that person to repent. In *The Miracle of Forgiveness,* Spencer W. Kimball states, "As the transgressor moves deeper and deeper in his sin, and the error is entrenched more deeply and the will to change is weakened, it becomes increasingly near-hopeless, and he skids down and down until either he does not want to climb back or he has lost the power to do so."[2]

All people sin and are therefore unclean to the extent to which they have sinned. President Marion G. Romney said, "Every person who has reached the age of accountability, except Jesus, has yielded in some degree to sin, some more and some less, but all save Jesus only have yielded sufficiently to be barred from the presence of God."[3]

President David O. McKay taught that "man has a dual nature: one, related to the earthly or animal life; the other, akin to the divine."[4] Each day we must fight the battle between our fallen, temporal nature and our spiritual nature. The Savior said of his sleeping apostles in Gethsemane, "The spirit indeed is willing, but the flesh is weak" (Matthew 26:41).

Our performance in keeping the commandments may be imperfect, but there is something to be said of having a willing spirit. And our Father in Heaven knows our hearts and our sincere desires.

When we sin, we lose the Spirit. According to George Q. Cannon, the Holy Ghost is grieved and withdraws from a person in sin, but "this does not take place all at once. Rarely is the Spirit entirely withdrawn in a moment."[5] The real problem comes when one does not want to repent or loses the will to repent. Elder M. Russell Ballard warned that "one of the great dangers of sin is its natural antipathy for the process of change." He said, "Sin blinds our eyes to eternal views and deafens our ears to the whisperings of the Holy Spirit. Each unrepented sin places additional distance between sinner and Savior and allows Satan better access to the sin-bound soul."[6]

During the closing days of the Nephite civilization the prophet Mormon had a brief hope for his people when he saw their sorrowing because he supposed it would lead to repentance. He unhappily learned that theirs was "the sorrowing of the damned, because the Lord would not always suffer them to take happiness in sin" (Mormon 2:13). When people have no *desire* to repent, they gradually lose the *power* to repent. In his book *The Miracle of Forgiveness,* President Kimball wrote, "Serious sin brings loss of this power, for the sinner then almost invariably cuts himself off from Church association and the influences that come from association with people who are striving for righteousness."[7]

The unrepentant sinner loses the Spirit and can ultimately lose the desire to repent. George Q. Cannon compared the loss of the Spirit to the setting sun, which disappears beyond the mountains and beneath the horizon, allowing darkness to spread. "So it is with the Spirit of the Lord. Being grieved and offended, and there being no repentance, it gradually withdraws itself from the soul, until darkness takes possession, and the man is left then to whatever influence and spirit he has yielded to."[8]

A sinner with no sincere desire to repent is on the road to apostasy. The more serious the sin, the faster he is traveling down that road.

Immorality is often a cause of apostasy from the Church. President George Q. Cannon said, "There has been no greater cause of apostasy in this Church than the want of virtue. You can predict the future of a man who is guilty of sins of this kind, unless he repents, as sure as you can predict that darkness will follow the setting of the sun."[9]

There are numerous examples from Church history of people who have lost their testimonies and become apostates because of serious transgressions, particularly immorality. Consider the case study of William E. McLellin. McLellin was baptized and ordained an elder in August 1831. He served as a successful missionary and in February 1835 was called to serve as a member of the first Quorum of the Twelve in this dispensation. Surprisingly, it was not long after his call to be an apostle that he fell away from the Church.

McLellin wrote a letter of membership withdrawal to Church leaders in August 1836. Concerted efforts were made by the leaders of the Church to persuade McLellin to come back, to which he responded positively. He and his family moved to Missouri to join the Church members living there. But his return to the Church and to his position in the Twelve was short lived.

William E. McLellin was officially excommunicated from the Church in May 1838. At his Church hearing, what we would today call a disciplinary council, McLellin went so far as to blame Church leaders for his apostasy and for his transgressions. He said that his lack of confidence in the Presidency of the Church had caused him to quit praying and keeping the commandments of God, which led him to indulge in sinful lusts.[10]

McLellin was excommunicated and left the Church, but he could not leave it alone. He began to take an active part in the persecution of the Saints in northern Missouri. An armed William E. McLellin was among the soldiers in the militia that arrested Joseph Smith and others near Far West, Missouri. Witnesses in Far West testified that after Joseph's arrest McLellin had entered Joseph Smith's home and had stolen some valuable articles.[11]

Evidently, McLellin was even present when the Prophet Joseph had his preliminary hearing in Richmond, Missouri. The following comes from an article in the *Millennial Star*:

> McLellin, who was a large and active man, went to the sheriff and asked for the privilege of flogging the Prophet. Permission was granted on condition that Joseph would fight. The sheriff made known to Joseph McLellin's earnest request, to which Joseph consented, if his irons were taken off. McLellin then refused to fight unless he could have a club, to which Joseph was perfectly willing; but the sheriff would not allow them to fight on such unequal terms.[12]

Heber C. Kimball reported his encounter with William E. McLellin, which took place about the time of the Prophet's arrest and as the Saints were being forced from their homes in Missouri. According to Kimball's account, McLellin approached him and said, "What do you think of the fallen prophet now? Has he not led you blindfolded long enough? Look and see yourself, poor, your family stripped and robbed, and your brethren in the same fix; are you satisfied with Joseph?"

Heber C. Kimball replied, "Yes, I am more satisfied with him a hundred-fold than ever I was before, for I see you in the very position that he foretold you would be in; a Judas to betray your brethren, if you did not forsake your adultery, fornication, lying and abominations."[13]

Another example of serious moral transgressions being responsible for someone's personal apostasy is Doctor Philastus Hurlbut. Philastus Hurlbut was not really a doctor. His given name was "Doctor," likely bestowed by his parents to inspire respect. He had been a member of the Methodist Church but had lost his membership with the Methodists because of adultery.

Hurlbut joined the restoration movement and became a Latter-day Saint in the spring of 1833. Shortly thereafter he served as a missionary for the Church in the eastern states. But it was not long before Hurlbut's immorality again caused him problems, and he was soon excommunicated from the Church. On June 3, 1833 a council of high priests, after listening to Hurlbut's confession, reinstated him as a member of the Church. But three weeks later he was excommunicated again.

Hurlbut became a bitter anti-Mormon and was actually hired to find and compile information that would be damaging to the Prophet Joseph Smith. When he threatened Joseph's life, swearing that he would wash his hands in Joseph Smith's blood, Hurlbut was arrested. He was brought to trial for his death threats upon Joseph Smith in March of 1834. The court issued a six-month restraining order on Hurlbut to keep him from harming the Prophet or his property.

Seeking information that would discredit the Prophet, Hurlbut traveled to New York to interview people who had known Joseph Smith and his family. Historian Milton V. Backman, Jr., wrote:

> A number of the affidavits specifically stated that Joseph Smith and members of his family were "indolent," "lazy," "intemperant," "money digger," "addicted to various habits," and "entirely destitute of moral character." . . . A legal investigation of the accusation of the Palmyra settlers exposed many inconsistencies in the affidavits. Most of the accusations were vague, undocumented, and unsubstantiated. The so-called witnesses relied on hearsay information or assumptions.[14]

Because of the immorality and the arrest for threatening Joseph's life, Hurlbut's own reputation suffered to the degree that the promoters of what would have been his book decided to have it released with a different author, E. D. Howe. *Mormonism Unvailed* was the first anti-Mormon book published. The author was listed as E. D. Howe, but the research and compilation was done by apostate Doctor Philastus Hurlbut.

One final example of unrepented serious transgression and apostasy is John C. Bennett. Whether Bennett's motives for coming to Nauvoo and uniting with the Church were ambition and self-promotion or a sincere desire to help build the kingdom is not known. John Taylor did not believe that Bennett's motives were completely corrupt, stating: "Respecting John C. Bennett I was well acquainted with him. At one time he was a good man."[15]

Whatever the reason, Bennett joined The Church of Jesus Christ of Latter-day Saints in 1840 and experienced a meteoric rise of influence and power, both politically and in the Church.[16] Because of the important role he played in getting the Illinois state government to pass the Nauvoo city charter, Bennett was elected as Nauvoo's first mayor in February 1841. Later that year, Bennett was called to serve in Sidney Rigdon's place in the First Presidency until the ailing Rigdon's health was restored.

Bennett came to Nauvoo professing to be an eligible bachelor, but it was rumored that he had a wife and family in Ohio. In June 1841 a letter sent to Joseph Smith from his brother, Hyrum, and William Law confirmed the suspicions of some that Bennett was, indeed, married; it also raised some other concerns about Bennett's questionable character.

Joseph confronted Bennett with the facts he had received, to which Bennett admitted that the information was true. Bennett appeared to be contrite, and Joseph gave him an opportunity to repent and get his life in order. Behind the scenes, however, he committed adultery with a number of women in Nauvoo. He introduced to them a doctrine he called "spiritual wifery," convincing these married women that although they may be married temporally to other men, they were "spiritually" married to him. He persuaded them to believe that they could have sexual relations with him because of this secret doctrine approved by the Prophet Joseph himself. Some believed him because, after all, Bennett was a member of the First Presidency.

Rumors of what Bennett was doing eventually got back to the Prophet Joseph. He issued a statement to be read by Emma Smith to the sisters of the Relief Society stating: "We do not want any one to believe any thing as coming from us, contrary to the old established morals & virtues . . . and all persons pretending to be authorized by us . . . whether they be prophets, Seers, or revelators; Patriarchs, Twelve Apostles, Elders, Priests, *Majors, Generals, . . . Lord Mayors* or the Devil, are alike culpable & shall be damned for such evil practices."[17]

It is likely that John C. Bennett knew that his time as a confidant of Joseph Smith and as an LDS leader and civic leader in Nauvoo was about to end. Joseph Smith even suspected that Bennett tried to assassinate him at a mock battle staged by the Nauvoo Legion in May 1842.

In Joseph's journal it reads:

> And if General Bennett's true feelings toward me are not made manifest to the world in a very short time, then it may be possible that the gentle breathings of that Spirit, which whispered to me on parade, that there was mischief concealed in that sham battle, were false; a short time will determine the point. Let John C. Bennett answer at the day of judgment, "Why did you request me to command one of the cohorts, and also to take my position without my staff, during the sham battle, on the 7th of May, 1842, where my life might have been the forfeit, and no man have known who did the deed?"[18]

Church disciplinary proceedings began on May 15, 1842, to determine what to do with John C. Bennett. He was accused of numerous things, such as frequenting a brothel and performing abortions. While unsure of the veracity of some of these accusations, the illicit sexual relations were confirmed. Two days after the proceedings began Bennett resigned as mayor of Nauvoo.

In a meeting with the Nauvoo city council John C. Bennett solemnly swore that Joseph Smith had never given him in public or in private any such authority to do the immoral things he had done. He also said, "I publicly avow that any one who has said that I have stated that General Joseph Smith had given me authority to hold illicit intercourse with women, is a liar in the face of God."[19]

Bennett was disfellowshipped on May 25, 1842, and subsequently excommunicated, although he would later say that he withdrew his own name from membership in the Church on the day that he resigned as mayor. He likely left Nauvoo sometime in the middle of June 1842. After leaving Nauvoo, Bennett toured the area, attacking Joseph Smith and Mormonism.

According to historian Ivan J. Barrett:

> Bennett had gone too far in sin to turn back; disgraced and pitied, he left Nauvoo and joined some of the Saints' former persecutors in Missouri, threatening the destruction of all his former brethren and conspiring with the Missourians to come to Nauvoo

> and kidnap the Prophet. . . . Bennett published a book under the title *The History of the Saints; or an Expose of Joe Smith and Mormonism.* In this ribald volume he says he joined the Mormon Church only to expose its treasonable designs and the unchaste practices of Joseph Smith and other leading Mormons.[20]

Of John C. Bennett, Andrew Skinner wrote, "Tragically, the kingdom-building efforts at Nauvoo produced a number of insiders-turned-outsiders, men who played a significant role in bringing to pass the martyrdom of the Prophet Joseph Smith and his brother Hyrum. Not the least of them was John C. Bennett."[21]

I once heard a man tell of a conversation he had with an anti-Mormon apostate from the Church. The former Latter-day Saint ranted about the inconsistencies and cover-ups of Church history and the despotic nature of Church leaders. After a few minutes the Church member interrupted the tirade and said, "Can I ask you just one question? Which of the commandments couldn't you live?" People who leave the Church in bitterness may voice many excuses for abandoning their faith, but in many cases the real reason is disobedience to commandments for which they choose not to repent.

In 1858 Apostle George A. Smith said, "I believe, if you will take the whole circle of the history of apostates from this Church, that in ninety-nine out of every hundred you will find that the spirit of adultery or covetousness was the original cause."[22]

NOTES

1. Smith, *Doctrines of Salvation,* 3:309.
2. Kimball, *The Miracle of Forgiveness,* 117.
3. Marion G. Romney, "Jesus—Savior and Redeemer," *BYU Speeches of the Year 1978,* 11.
4. McKay, *Pathways to Happiness,* 163.
5. Cannon, *Gospel Truth,* 2:265.
6. Ballard, *When Thou Art Converted,* 32.
7. Kimball, *The Miracle of Forgiveness,* 324.
8. Cannon, *Gospel Truth,* 2:266.
9. George Q. Cannon, in *Collected Discourses,* vol. 2, 117–18.

10. "History of Brigham Young," *Millennial Star,* vol. 26, no. 51, 17 Dec. 1864, 808.
11. Shipps and Welch, *The Journals of William E. McLellin,* 326–327, footnote 191.
12. "History of Brigham Young," *Millennial Star,* 808.
13. Whitney, *Life of Heber C. Kimball,* 218.
14. Backman, *Heavens Resound,* 202–203.
15. Smith, *History of the Church,* 5:81.
16. Questions often arise as to why the Prophet Joseph Smith would allow a corrupt man to hold positions of leadership, not only in government, but also in the Church. Because this study does not really focus on that aspect of the Bennett story I would suggest the article, "John C. Bennett: For Prophet or Profit?" by Andrew Skinner, found in *Regional Studies in Latter-day Saint Church History: Illinois.*
17. Quoted in Richard S. Van Wagoner, "Sarah M. Pratt: The Shaping of an Apostate," *Dialogue: A Journal of Mormon Thought,* vol. 19, no. 2, Summer 1986, 74. Emphasis added. Bennett was a Major General in the Nauvoo Legion and the Mayor of Nauvoo. Skinner suggests that the positioning of the words Major and General were purposely placed by Joseph because of Bennett's title in the Legion. Skinner, "John C. Bennett: For Prophet or Profit?" in *Regional Studies in Latter-day Saint Church History: Illinois,* H. Dean Garrett, ed. (Provo, UT: Brigham Young University, 1995), 257.
18. Smith, *History of the Church,* 5:4.
19. Roberts, *Comprehensive History of the Church,* vol. 2, 142.
20. Barrett, *Joseph Smith and the Restoration,* 517.
21. Skinner, "John C. Bennett: For Prophet or Profit?" in *Regional Studies in Latter-day Saint Church History: Illinois,* 249.
22. George Albert Smith, in *Journal of Discourses,* 7:114.

6

Finding Fault and Murmuring

I know of very few people who are not guilty of fault finding or murmuring to one degree or another. Think about it. How many of you have never, ever complained about or criticized a Church leader or a Church program?

"I don't know what the bishop was thinking when he called me to this position."

"The elders quorum president is big on delegation, but he doesn't actually do much of the work."

"Why is our stake president so long-winded? This is the third time in a row that our meetings have gone overtime."

"Don't get me wrong; I follow the Presidency of the Church, but I just think they ought to stay out of this issue."

Sound familiar?

Fault finding and murmuring are dangerous because they *are* so common and also because a person who is finding fault and murmuring believes that he is seeing things correctly and actually has the *right* to complain. In reality, the sin of fault finding has very little to do with the actions or person being complained about. Maybe the elders quorum president doesn't work as hard as those he is assigning responsibilities. Perhaps three meetings in a row have gone over the scheduled time because the stake president spoke longer than he had intended. If these problems do exist, they are for the elders quorum president or stake president to overcome. Fault finding will not correct the situation, and murmuring certainly does not help because these things come from the spirit of pride and contention. The Lord was clear that "the spirit of contention is not of me, but is of the devil, who is the father of contention" (3 Nephi 11:29).

President Gordon B. Hinckley remarked that just like in Nauvoo in the early days of the Church, we still have those who "profess membership but spend much of their time in criticizing, in finding fault, and in looking for defects in the Church, in its leaders, in its programs." He continued, "They contribute nothing to the building of the kingdom. They rationalize their efforts, trying to justify with pretenses of doing good for the cause, but the result of those efforts is largely only a fragmentation of faith, their own and that of others."[1]

Moses told the murmuring children of Israel that the Lord heard their murmurings for "your murmurings are not against us, but against the Lord" (Exodus 16:8). The direction given in scripture and by latter-day prophets to avoid criticism of Church leaders is not to protect the leaders. Elder Dallin H. Oaks said:

> The counsel against speaking evil of Church leaders is not so much for the benefit of the leaders as it is for the spiritual well-being of members who are prone to murmur and find fault. The Church leaders I know are durable people. They made their way successfully in a world of unrestrained criticism before they reached their current callings. They have no personal need for protection; they seek no personal immunities from criticism—constructive or destructive. They only seek to declare what they understand to be the word of the Lord to his people.[2]

In our fallen state, it does not take much to cause many people to voice their disappointment or discouragement. Even the best of God's children have sometimes fallen into this trap. Book of Mormon matriarch Sariah was so concerned because her sons had not returned from Jerusalem that she criticized her husband, Lehi. She complained about the family's situation, saying, "Behold thou hast led us forth from the land of our inheritance, and my sons are no more, and we perish in the wilderness" (1 Nephi 5:2). Even the great prophet Lehi "began to murmur against the Lord his God" because of the sufferings of his family in the wilderness (1 Nephi 16:20).

Because murmuring, fault finding, and criticism are so common among fallen man, even in the Church, it must be pointed out that these things alone typically do not lead to apostasy from the Lord's kingdom. Clearly, the vast majority of Latter-day Saints who have on occasion murmured or found fault with Church programs, local Church leaders, or even general authorities have not become apostates. But when we criticize and complain we are literally taking steps down the road toward apostasy. Unless we overcome our telestial tendency to complain, it can eventually lead us completely out of the Church.

Boyd K. Packer wrote, "If one becomes critical and harbors negative feelings, the Spirit will withdraw. Only when they repent will the Spirit return. My experience is that the channels of inspiration always follow that order. You are safe following your leaders."[3] And Harold B. Lee stated that "those who criticize the leaders of this Church are showing signs of a spiritual sickness which, unless curbed, will bring about eventually spiritual death."[4]

Expressed negativism can sow seeds of doubt in others as well. Criticism can result in a loss of faith, not only of the one complaining, but also of others. As Neal A. Maxwell wrote, "Those who are lukewarm usually cool down the faith of others; the Church member who is half-informed and half-committed may quarter the faith of the weak."[5] I think of some people that I know who have become bitter toward the Church and have been extremely vocal in their bitterness. I have witnessed the damage they have done to their own children. How many generations will be negatively affected by an individual's departure from light and truth?

There are many examples from our Church history of individuals in the Church who became disgruntled with a particular policy, a newly revealed doctrine, or a Church leader, and began criticizing the Church, first privately and then publicly. Many of these critics became embittered and ultimately left the Church. Some, like Oliver Cowdery and

Martin Harris, eventually found their way back into the faith. Some were not so fortunate.

William S. Godbe, E. L. T. Harrison, and Edward Tullidge were members of the Church who, in the 1860s and 70s, became extremely irritated with Brigham Young's economic plans for the Utah Territory. They were all merchants and businessmen and did not like Brigham Young interfering with temporal and economic issues. They had above-average education and literary skills and were acquainted with the intellectual ideas of that time.

They, and others, met to discuss the Church's policies and doctrines and share their increasing skepticism of Mormonism. This private murmuring led to public complaints as they began to publish the very critical *Utah Magazine*.

In addition to their complaints about Brigham Young's economic policies, they were also bothered because they felt there weren't enough spiritual experiences within Mormonism. Each of these men had experienced spiritual manifestations as part of the conversion process at the time they had joined with the Church. They wanted spiritual experiences to continue, but at an accelerated rate. Spiritually immature, they did not understand that mortal man cannot force spiritual things. Also, it did not occur to them that the absence of spiritual experiences in their lives had to do with their own lack of faith, their disobedience, and their criticism of the Lord's anointed. Instead, they came to believe that it was Mormonism that stifled their spiritual growth as well as their economic freedom.

In order to enhance what they considered to be spiritual growth and to increase the number of "spiritual" experiences, they got involved with spiritualism, séances, and communing with the dead. They began their own Church of Zion, commonly known as Godbeites.

The Godbeites were comprised of disaffected Mormons who saw themselves as free-thinking intellectuals, "and not surprisingly their spiritualist experiences confirmed their religious doubts."[6] Their journey from believers in the restoration of the gospel to being critical of Church leaders and finally becoming apostates who created their own religion took them far, far away from true doctrine. They forsook their belief in the Atonement of Christ and His Second Coming. They did not believe in a physical resurrection or in a literal devil.

Within a few short years their new movement was gone, but not before they led away a number of Latter-day Saints, including the first British convert to the Church, George Watt, and Apostle Amasa Lyman. What had begun with a few disgruntled men finding fault with Church leaders ended in an apostate movement that took a number of Church members and leaders with it.[7]

Will there be times when a person in a leadership position in the Church makes a mistake or handles a situation incorrectly? Of course, this will inevitably happen. All members of the Church, including its leaders, have made errors before and will again. It is the nature of fallen man to be imperfect. There has only been one perfect person who ever lived on this earth—the Lord Jesus Christ. The rest of us are guilty to one degree or another of doing things wrong.

We have been admonished not to find fault or murmur. So what are we to do if we believe that one of our leaders, or anyone else for that matter, is in error? We first need to ask ourselves, "How serious is this mistake? Does it really matter?" A stake president got my name wrong as he introduced me to speak at stake conference. A bishop unjustly chastised a friend of mine in a ward council meeting one Sunday morning. Are these blunders sufficient to cause bitter feelings or to result in a loss of faith?

I had been a member of a particular ward for about four years and had even served in the bishopric of that ward. One Sunday morning I was greeted by a Church leader as I came into sacrament meeting with, "How are you doing this morning, Roger?" I was surprised because my name is Richard and I thought this man knew me pretty well. I suppose I could have felt hurt or insulted, but honestly, what did it matter? I probably should have let it slide completely, but I decided to have a little fun. I said, "I'm doing great, Bob!" He looked bewildered and said, "My name's not Bob." I replied, "My name's not Roger." He apologized; so did I, and we had a good laugh.

But what if we believe a Church leader has made a serious mistake, and we think it does matter? Then, we need to go through the proper channels to deal with the situation. In some cases, we might want to go directly to the person we believe to be in error to discuss and clarify the situation. The person may recognize his error, or we may find out that we did not know the whole story and have misjudged the person. That may be all that is needed.

If we feel that approaching the person in error would be inappropriate, we then follow the proper procedure and go to the individual who has stewardship for the person with whom we are having a problem. For a counselor in a bishopric, we can go to the bishop. For a bishop, we can go to our stake president.

Even though the proper channels are in place, I believe it would be a rare occurrence to go over someone's head. This should be reserved for something serious. Usually, if we feel we have been slighted or mistreated or misunderstood, it is a pride issue on our part or a simple mistake made with no malice.

Finally, if there has been an error made, perceived or real, we should keep our mouths shut, except to those we absolutely have to speak to as we go through proper ecclesiastical channels. No one else needs to know. No one else should know. Elder George F. Richards once said, "When we say anything bad about the leaders of the Church, whether true or false, we tend to impair their influence and their usefulness and are thus working against the Lord and his cause."[8]

I was sitting in a meeting where it was announced that an individual had just been called to a position of leadership within the stake where I lived. No sooner did they announce the name than the murmuring commenced. "Why would they choose him? I don't think that he is right for the job. There are so many others who are more qualified than he is."

Although I did not say anything to anyone, the thought did occur to me that he was not exactly perfect for that position in the Church. At that moment the memory of an experience I had at scout camp years before flashed through my mind. I was puzzled as to why my mind would recall that particular incident, but it soon made sense to me.

The summer after I turned twelve I went with the Boy Scouts to Camp Maple Dell for a week. The day after we arrived, camp leaders met with the scouts from each camp to explain a problem the camp was facing and elicit their help. They told us that the camp was being overrun with porcupines that were damaging many of the trees in the area. The scout leaders said that if we came across a porcupine during our stay at Camp Maple Dell, we were to dispatch it immediately.

We began to find clubs that we could use if we happened upon a porcupine while we were hiking. Even though no one in the entire camp saw a porcupine during that week, an interesting phenomenon did take place as the week progressed. Porcupines were forgotten, but a contest as to who had the best club emerged. Scouts sanded and carved words, pictures, and designs on their clubs. I was caught up in "club fever" and spent several hours scouring the woods for the perfect dead-fall branch with which to make my club. Each time I thought I'd found one that was just right, I'd pick it up and find that it wasn't as straight as I wanted or as thick as I needed. Some limbs were too big. Others were covered with dirt or mud. It only took me a few hours to realize that I was not going to find a perfectly made Louisville Slugger lying in the forest. What I needed to do was to find a piece of wood that I could work with until it was the way I wanted it.

It was not until the moment I was sitting in a Church meeting that this experience I had at scout camp became a meaningful parable for me. When I was walking through the forest looking for the perfect club, many looked promising until I picked them up and examined them carefully. Each time I saw flaws; things that were imperfect.

Was the man they had just called perfect for that leadership position? Who is perfect for any calling? If another person had been selected out of the congregation and called to that position instead of the first man, would people have noticed the other person's flaws and would there have been some murmuring? Just as there are no Louisville Sluggers lying in the woods, so there are no perfect people with whom Heavenly Father can staff His Church. There are only people with the potential of being right for the job as God works with them and smoothes rough edges. I remember my wife's comments from the pulpit when I was called to be a bishop. She said, "I have a perfect knowledge that Rich will be an imperfect bishop. But I know that he will do his best to follow the Spirit."

As imperfect beings, we simply cannot afford to criticize, find fault, and murmur. Joseph Smith told the Saints "not to follow the example of the adversary in accusing the brethren." He continued, "If you will not accuse me, I will not accuse you. If you throw a cloak of charity over my sins, I will over yours."[9]

Even though mistakes will be made, they will typically not be severe. We should be at peace concerning the leadership of each of our prophets for we know that God would not allow his prophets to lead His people off the path of righteousness. Wilford Woodruff stated, "The Lord will never permit me or any other man who stands as President of this Church to lead you astray. . . . If I were to attempt that, the Lord would remove me out of my place."[10]

There is a great statement by Joseph Smith concerning those who find fault with the Church. He said: "I will give you one of the Keys of the mysteries of the Kingdom. It is an eternal principle, that has existed with God from all eternity: That man who rises up to condemn others, finding fault with the Church, saying that they are out of the way, while he himself is righteous, then know assuredly, that that man is in the high road to apostasy; and if he does not repent, will apostatize, as God lives."[11]

NOTES

1. Gordon B. Hinckley, "Dedication of the John Taylor Building," *BYU 1982–83 Fireside and Devotional Speeches*, 18.
2. Dallin H. Oaks, "Criticism," *Ensign*, February, 1987, 70.
3. Boyd K. Packer, "Personal Revelation: The Gift, the Test, and the Promise," *Ensign*, November 1994, 61.
4. Harold B. Lee, *Conference Report*, October 1947, 67.
5. Maxwell, *Meek and Lowly*, 6.
6. Ronald W. Walker, "When the Spirits Did Abound: Nineteenth-Century Utah's Encounter with Free-Thought Radicalism," *Utah Historical Quarterly*, vol. 50, number 4, 306.
7. Information about the Godbeites was taken from Walker, *Wayward Saints:*

Godbeites and Brigham Young; and Ronald W. Walker, "When the Spirits Did Abound: Nineteenth-Century Utah's Encounter with Free-Thought Radicalism," *Utah Historical Quarterly,* vol. 50, no. 4, 305–324.

8. George F. Richards, *Conference Report,* April 1947, 24.
9. Smith, *History of the Church,* 4:445.
10. "Excerpts from Three Addresses by President Wilford Woodruff Regarding the Manifesto," found in Official Declaration—1, Doctrine and Covenants, 292.
11. Smith, *History of the Church,* 3:385.

7

STEADYING THE ARK

The notion of "steadying the ark" comes from the story found in 2 Samuel where a man named Uzzah put forth his hand to keep the Ark of the Covenant from tipping over. "Uzzah put forth his hand to the ark of God, and took hold of it; for the oxen shook it. And the anger of the Lord was kindled against Uzzah; and God smote him there for his error; and there he died by the ark of God" (2 Samuel 6:6–7).

I remember first becoming aware of this story and how unfair I thought it was that Uzzah was punished severely for just trying to help. I guess I had not completely thought this through because it was the Lord who did the punishing, and so we can rest assured that what happened to Uzzah was not unjust. In section 85 of the Doctrine and Covenants the Lord again puts "steadying the ark" in a negative connotation.

Steadying the ark is actually an extension of fault finding. Instead of only complaining and criticizing, an "ark steadier" sees what he believes to be an error and, acting without authority, tries to correct the perceived error by taking matters into his own hands.

An ark steadier may have good intentions but has clouded vision because of pride. Uzzah may have meant well. We cannot judge Uzzah's intentions or his heart. Only God can do that. But his actions might reveal his lack of faith in the Lord's ability or power to handle the situation.

My brother-in-law had an interesting experience with a member of the Church who expressed his lack of confidence in the prophet and apostles. The man then added, "Most Church members don't have faith in Christ at all. They simply put their faith in the leaders of the Church. And it appears to me that with so many like-minded men in leadership positions, the Lord is not able to get the men he would really like to serve into those positions of authority." Incidentally, the man speaking felt that he should be in a leadership position but had been passed over by the "uninspired men in power."

My brother-in-law responded, "If you think that the Lord cannot get the people He really wants into callings of authority, then it is you who do not have any faith in Christ."

Like fault finding, this step on the road to apostasy is very common. Most likely every ward in the Church has its "ark steadiers." I am familiar with a situation that took place in a ward many years ago. A new Relief Society president had been called and her name presented to the congregation for a sustaining vote. After sacrament meeting, another woman approached the bishop and insisted on speaking with him privately and immediately.

She told the bishop that she had received a revelation a few weeks earlier informing her that she was to be the new Relief Society president. She said that the bishopric had made a mistake. Then, she actually said to the bishop, "Now, you need to release her and put me in." The bishop replied, "You may have received a revelation that you will be a Relief Society president, but it is not now. The right person received the call. You need to let this go, live faithfully, and wait for the Lord to call you through proper channels."

And before I point the finger too far away from home, awhile back the bishop of my ward was a very close friend of mine. I thought he made a mistake in calling a certain person to be the Gospel Doctrine teacher. I did not say anything to him at the time. But as weeks went by I became more and more agitated at what was being taught in the Sunday School class. For a couple of weeks I made a list of every false doctrine and incorrect thing that this person taught, and then after church meetings one day I took my list into the bishop's office to report my findings.

The bishop took the notebook, looked over it carefully, smiled, and said, "Well, this is very interesting. I appreciate all the work you've done, especially since I don't remember calling you to be the 'Sheriff of the Sunday School.'" I took the notebook back, ripped the list out, threw it away, and said, "Sorry."

I felt pretty foolish and was appreciative when he shared with me an experience he had with the bishop before him. He said that he felt the need to inform the bishop about a particular situation in the ward. The previous bishop politely thanked him and said that he was already aware of it. My friend then inquired what the bishop was going to do and why hadn't anything been done already. My friend told me that the former bishop was kind, but firm, in letting him know that it was being taken care of and that it was really none of his concern.

I do believe there may be some things we might need to bring to our priesthood leaders' awareness. But we need to be guided by the Spirit, go through proper channels, and once they are informed, we need to back off and let them handle it.

We should avoid even the desire to steady the ark. If unchecked, steadying the ark can lead to apostasy. President David O. McKay said, "Look around us and see how quickly men who attempt to unauthoritatively steady the ark die spiritually. Their souls become embittered, their minds distorted, their judgment faulty, and their spirit depressed."[1]

As President of the Church, Brigham Young experienced his share of those who were trying to steady the ark. He said: "Let the kingdom alone, the Lord steadies the ark; and if it does jostle, and appear to need steadying, if the way is a little sideling sometimes, and to all appearance threatens its overthrow, be careful how you stretch forth your hands to steady it; let us not be too officious in meddling with that which does not concern us; let it alone, it is the Lord's work. I know enough to let the kingdom alone, and do my duty. It carries me, I do not carry the kingdom."[2]

An apocryphal story about Brigham Young gives us an inkling of how he may have felt about those who tried to steady the ark. According to the anecdote, early one morning a man rode his horse into Salt Lake City to see Brother Brigham. He was told by President Young's secretary, William Clayton, that even though Brigham would arrive in a few minutes, he had not been feeling well and it would be better if the man did not try to see him.

"But I must see him! I have a message which I must deliver in person!" said the man.

Brigham Young arrived shortly after that and was informed by Brother Clayton that the man had ridden from Bountiful that morning with what he said was an important message.

"Well, what is it?" Brigham asked.

The man replied, "An angel of the Lord came to me last night and gave me a message for the welfare of the church which I am to deliver to you in private."

Brigham Young looked the man in the eye and said, "Now you just ride along back to Bountiful. And if the angel comes to you again with a message for me you tell him that I said to go to hell because that is where he came from!"[3]

To give an example of how steadying the ark can lead one out of the Church, let me share the story of George Hinkle. Hinkle joined the Church in 1832 and shortly thereafter went on a mission. Among the people he taught and baptized was future apostle, Charles C. Rich. Later, Hinkle was called to be a branch president and then became a member of a high council.

In Missouri, Hinkle rose to the rank of colonel in the Missouri state militia. The Saints had been kicked out of Jackson County in the latter part of 1833. By the autumn of 1838 most members of the Church in Missouri were living in Daviess and Caldwell counties. But hostilities arose again between the Missourians and the Mormons. The Militia was ordered to keep peace between the two groups and, initially, to protect the Mormons from mob action. However, because of various false reports that Governor Boggs received, he became convinced that the Mormons were guilty of sedition. On October 27, 1838, Governor

Boggs issued the "extermination order." The Haun's Mill Massacre happened three days later. Mormon troops were on the alert for further mob action.

George Hinkle was the highest ranking officer of the militia who at that time were assigned to protect the Saints of Far West, Missouri. When he met with General Lucas and other commanders of the Missouri state militia, they showed him the extermination orders they had received from Governor Boggs. Lucas assured Colonel Hinkle that the militia would go easy on the Mormons if they met the terms of surrender. These terms included giving up all weapons and turning Church leaders over to state officials to be tried and punished.

Hinkle went back to the Mormon encampment and told Joseph that the militia officers wanted to talk to him and certain other brethren in order to settle the difficulties without bloodshed. Joseph and other Church leaders agreed to accompany Hinkle to the militia camp. When they got there Hinkle announced to Lucas: "Here, general, are the prisoners I agreed to deliver to you."[4]

I suppose that Hinkle believed he was saving the Saints from extermination. But he did not consult Joseph Smith or other Church leaders. Instead, he made a secret deal with militia leaders on behalf of the Church, when he had no authority to do so. Believing that he knew what was best for the Church, he tried to steady the ark.

Because of his actions, Hinkle was viewed as a betrayer of the Latter-days Saints. From some of his personal writings afterward, he appears to have actually been surprised by the reaction of the Mormon people. He claimed that he was not a traitor, but that he had become a scapegoat. Hinkle could not understand why the general membership of the Church was angry with him and why he was later excommunicated.

George Hinkle later founded his own church in June 1840, calling it The Church of Jesus Christ, the Bride the Lamb's Wife. It is reported that his church was like Mormonism with the Book of Mormon left out. After Joseph's death, Hinkle's group struggled for a time, and later merged with Sidney Rigdon's group.[5]

Another example of trying to steady the ark is the case of Lyman Wight. Wight was a member of the Quorum of Twelve during Joseph Smith's ministry. Before Joseph died, he and Wight discussed various possibilities of where the Saints might go if they were forced to leave Nauvoo. Wight advocated moving to the southwest.

After Joseph Smith's martyrdom, Wight was not one of those who tried to assert himself and become the leader of the Church. He initially supported the leadership of Brigham Young and the Twelve. But Wight had his own ideas as to what path the Church should follow, which differed from the rest of the Twelve. He tried to convince Brigham Young to sanction the plan of southwest colonization, but the Twelve had made different plans.

In 1845 Lyman Wight took a group of about one hundred fifty Latter-day Saints to Texas. He saw himself as following through on an assignment given him by the Prophet Joseph. He refused to acknowledge the instructions of Brigham Young and the other leaders of the Church at the time.

In 1848 Brigham Young said of Wight, "He has been from us a good while; we feel yet to hold on to him; we have faith to hold on and not give him up. We hope he will come back and do a good work."[6] Missionaries were sent from Salt Lake City to persuade Wight and his followers to return to the faith but were unsuccessful because of strong feelings of opposition toward Brigham Young and the Twelve. Ultimately, Lyman Wight not only lost his place in the Quorum of the Twelve but was also excommunicated from the Church in 1849.

Here was a man in a very responsible leadership position who believed he knew what the Church ought to do. Those in authority over him could not persuade him otherwise. He was trying to steady the ark —to take the Church in the direction he felt it should go, even though he did not have the authority to do so and was out of harmony with the leadership of the Church. He followed his own path and led a group of people away from the restored gospel. After his death, some of his followers found their way back to the gospel, but most returned to the Midwest and united with the Reorganized Church.[7]

Elder George A. Smith said that in the early history of our Church there was a prevalent spirit which prompted some "to suppose that they knew more than the Prophet." He continued, "Elders would tell you that the prophet was going wrong, men who thought they knew all about this work thirty or forty years some of them before the Lord revealed it, tried 'to steady the ark.' The Church was constantly afflicted with such a class of men."[8]

The Church is still afflicted with people who try to steady the ark. In most cases it is done by well meaning people and is fairly innocent in nature. However, steadying the ark is an act of pride which can cause problems within our wards and stakes. And, as we have seen, steadying the ark can lead to complete apostasy.

NOTES

1. McKay, *Pathways to Happiness,* 86.
2. Brigham Young, in *Journal of Discourses,* 11:252.
3. I have heard or read several versions of this story. One account is found in Fife, *Saints of Sage and Saddle: Folklore Among the Mormons,* 99–100.
4. Smith, *History of the Church,* 3:445.
5. Information about George Hinkle was taken from Smith, *History of the Church;* Shields, *Divergent Paths of the Restoration;* Rich, *Those Who Would Be Leader;* Garr and Johnson, ed., *Regional Studies in Latter-day Saint Church History: Missouri;* and from a letter written by George Hinkle to W. W. Phelps published in George Hinkle's church's newspaper *The Ensign,* vol. 1, number 2, August 1844 and vol. 1, number 9, March 1845.
6. Kate B. Carter, "Denominations That Base Their Belief on the Teachings of Joseph Smith," *Our Pioneer Heritage,* 5:347.
7. Information about Lyman Wight was taken from Shields, *Divergent Paths of the Restoration;* and Carter, "Denominations That Base Their Belief on the Teachings of Joseph Smith," *Our Pioneer Heritage,* 5:346–47.
8. George A. Smith, in *Journal of Discourses,* 11:7.

8

Desire for Wealth, Power, and Fame

As discussed earlier, pride is at the core of every negative attribute, ambition, and condition that can lead to apostasy; and the desire for wealth, power, and fame is one of the most universal manifestations of pride. The Apostle Paul wrote that "the love of money is the root of all evil" (1 Timothy 6:10). Moroni wrote to us who would live in the latter days, saying, "I speak unto you as if ye were present, and yet ye are not. But behold, Jesus Christ hath shown you unto me, and I know your doing" (Mormon 8:35). And what did Moroni witness as he was shown our world in the latter days? He saw people lifted up in the pride of their hearts, "unto the wearing of very fine apparel, unto envying, and strifes, and malice, and persecutions, and all manner of iniquities; . . . for behold, ye do love money and your substance" (Mormon 8:36–37).

Through the Prophet Joseph Smith the Lord has instructed us as to why many are called but few are chosen. He said that it was "because their hearts are set so much upon the things of this world, and aspire to the honors of men" (D&C 121:35). Joseph Smith further stated "that it is the nature and disposition of almost all men, as soon as they get a little authority, as they suppose, they will immediately begin to exercise unrighteous dominion" (D&C 121:39). I once heard a Church leader say that there were some occasions when he thought the word "almost" should be removed from the phrase "almost all men."

Thus we see that Church members are challenged and tempted with the rest of the world with the lure of power, wealth, and fame. Clearly, power, wealth, or fame, in and of themselves, are not evil. When we have an eye single to the glory of God, then these things can be great blessings in the building up of His kingdom. It is only when these things become the selfish focus of our desires that Satan can use them as tools to destroy us.

There are numerous examples from Church history in which individuals lost their testimonies and became apostates because their desires were selfish and they attempted to build their own kingdom rather than God's kingdom. Lorenzo Snow taught that:

> There were many to whom the Lord had revealed things and blessed them in many ways. But they could not withstand the temptations of the world. But they went to work and increased their wealth in a way that God was not pleased with. They grasped at every opportunity to get wealth in a way that was displeasing to the Almighty. Hence some of them apostatized in consequence of their indulging in that spirit. I wish to make these statements for the benefit of the Latter-day Saints. Listen to the whisperings of the Holy Spirit, that when such things are brought before us to tempt us we may have power to lay them one side.[1]

Charles B. Thompson joined the Church in 1835. After the death of Joseph and Hyrum Smith, Thompson supported Brigham Young and the Twelve until it was decided that the Latter-day Saints were to migrate west. He left the Church and became involved with James J. Strang's church for a time. Ultimately, Thompson started his own church, The Congregation of Jehovah's Presbytery of Zion, also known as the Conjespresites. Among his teachings, Thompson claimed that he was Ephraim reborn among the Gentiles.

Examining what was required to become a Conjespresite, it causes one to wonder if Thompson was more concerned about his financial well-being than the souls of his followers. Each convert to Thompson's church was required to take the following oath: "I now give, bequeath, and consecrate, and promise to pay to Charles B. Thompson, chief steward of the House of Jehovah, the chief teacher of the Order of Elias the Prophet, in Jehovah's Presbytery of Zion, for the service thereof, the value of one-tenth of my real and personal estate, including cash on hand and money due, and one-tenth of the increase of the remainder forever; also one-tenth of my time and services. And I solemnly covenant never to require any remuneration for the same."[2]

Although this might sound similar to the law of tithing found within The Church of Jesus Christ of Latter-day Saints, there are several not so subtle differences. Tithing is a free-will offering—a commandment, but not required to be a member of the Church. Also, we pay our tithing to the Church, while Conjespresites vowed to pay Charles B. Thompson.

But this was not all. Thompson, or Father Ephraim, had almost complete control over his followers. He required gift oblations and sacrifices as well as tithing. There were special gift days each year[3] when the faithful were to make their gift oblations to Thompson. In addition to tithing, special gifts on gift days, and fast offering, Thompson also instituted the Law of Sacrifices where members of his faith were required to execute to him bills of sale for all of their personal property and deed to him all their real property.

After a time, the members of The Congregation of Jehovah's Presbytery of Zion, "got wise" to Thompson's accumulation of their wealth. Thompson was forced to leave town, and though he never came back, he refused to relinquish title of the land back to the people. Eventually, they got their land back through the courts.

The story of Walter Murray Gibson is a fascinating case study of corruption, originating with a desire for power. Even before he had any contact with The Church of Jesus Christ of Latter-day Saints, Walter Murray Gibson was aware of the Mormons and their plight as they were forced out of Illinois. Gibson came up with a plan to relocate the Latter-day Saints to the islands of New Guinea. His plan for relocation was presented to several representatives of the Church and even to U. S. President James Buchanan. Gibson later traveled to Salt Lake City to meet and present his ideas directly to Brigham Young.

Gibson spent the winter with the Saints in the Salt Lake Valley, and in January 1860 he was baptized a member of the Church. After serving a brief mission to the eastern states, Gibson was sent by Brigham Young on a mission to Japan and Malaysia. He got as far as Hawaii and decided to stay there.

The Church had already been established in Hawaii, but the missionaries had been called home three years earlier, leaving the islands with no official Church representative. Gibson took advantage of the opportunity and quickly established himself as the leader of the Church in that area. He took upon himself not the title of mission president, but Chief President of the Islands of the Seas and of the Hawaiian Islands.

At a conference held for the Saints about a month after he arrived, Gibson took charge of the Church in Hawaii and announced that some changes were going to be made. He sold certificates of membership to those who wanted to remain active in the Church. He also sold offices in priesthood leadership, the higher the office, the more money it cost. He sold Aaronic Priesthood ordinations and Melchizedek Priesthood offices, including seventy, bishop, archbishop, Quorum of the Twelve, and First Presidency. He even sold an office for women called "priestess of the temple."

For the next three years, Gibson controlled the Church in Hawaii, requiring the Saints there to turn over all their substance to him: horses, sheep, goats, land, and so forth. Those who stayed in the Church became wholly dependent upon Gibson for food, clothing, and their very existence. Those who wished an audience with Gibson were required to enter the room on their hands and knees in order to approach the white-robed Gibson.

Some of the older members of the Church remembered what it had been like when previous LDS missionaries had presided in their land. Troubled by their new leader, they sent letters to Salt Lake City to inform the Church leaders there what was happening in their island home. In response, Brigham Young sent of group of men to investigate, including apostles Ezra T. Benson and Lorenzo Snow. Also in the group was former missionary to Hawaii, Joseph F. Smith.

When the brethren arrived in Hawaii, Gibson refused to turn over deeds to the lands he had received or purchased supposedly for the

Church, but had put in his name. Speaking of Gibson, Joseph F. Smith wrote: "He declared he should use his influence to keep the natives in his power . . . if he could, and that they should receive no benefit from the land they had bought only as they would become subject to him."[4]

Walter Murray Gibson was excommunicated from the Church and lost his influence over most of the Hawaiian Saints, but not before causing much damage to the faith of many of those early Church members in Hawaii.

Some newspapers of the time saw Gibson as a philanthropist and social reformer who improved the islanders' standard of living by building schools and hospitals. Others saw him as an exploiter of the Hawaiian people. There is no doubt that Walter Murray Gibson had dreams of power and authority. Consider the following lines from his own diary: "I view him [the Hawaiian] and treat him as an interesting yet feeble younger brother, a subject of an oceanic empire. . . . Who or what shall I fear where I am King—and . . . this is but the baby of my Kingdom."[5]

After his excommunication from the Church, Gibson remained in Hawaii for a time and went on to much of the temporal success he sought, even becoming the Prime Minister of the Kingdom of Hawaii. But as he sought for wealth, power, and even his own kingdom, he may find that he has lost his place in the kingdom of God.[6]

The next example, by comparison to the previous examples, is certainly not as severe, but it illustrates the point that the desire for wealth can cloud one's judgment, even to the extent of apostasy. William Law was a counselor to Joseph Smith in the First Presidency of the Church during the Nauvoo era. Law was also the owner of a mill in Nauvoo.

One day Bishop Smoot made a wager with George A. Smith that Willard Richards weighed more than George A. Smith. Incidentally, both Smith and Richards weighed more than three hundred pounds each. The three men went to William Law's mill to use the mill's scales to determine which man weighed more. There were two sets of scales; one for the weighing of incoming wheat and the other to weigh outgoing flour. They were surprised to discover that if they used the scale that was used to weigh incoming wheat; they were twelve pounds under their actual weight. If they used the scale that was used to weigh outgoing flour, each man was twelve pounds heavier than his actual weight. In other words, William Law was cheating people on both how much grain they were selling him and how much flour he was selling them.[7]

Law's dishonesty appears to have been only one aspect of his hypocrisy and pretended piety. Law later apostatized and, along with his brother and two other sets of brothers, began the Church of the Laws, Fosters, and Higbees. Essentially, their "religion" was to destroy the influence of Joseph Smith. Law became one of the individuals responsible for publishing the anti-Mormon *Nauvoo Expositor*. Filled with libelous accusations, the *Expositor* was subsequently destroyed by order of the Nauvoo City Council. This action eventually led to the arrest and murder of Joseph and Hyrum Smith.

The story of James J. Strang is one of the most amazing sagas in the early history of the Church. Strang became aware of the Latter-day Saints through his brother-in-law. Shortly thereafter, he traveled to Nauvoo to learn more about this new faith. On February 25, 1844, Strang was baptized by Joseph Smith in the font of the unfinished Nauvoo Temple. One week later Hyrum Smith conferred the Melchizedek Priesthood upon Strang and ordained him to the office of elder.

At that time persecution against the Saints was increasing in the state of Illinois, and Church leaders were considering other places to settle if the Latter-day Saints were forced to leave Nauvoo and the surrounding areas. Strang lived in Wisconsin and suggested the possibility of relocating the Church headquarters to Wisconsin. Church leaders requested him to return to his home state, survey the area for possible relocation, and submit a report, which he did. Strang also sent a letter to Joseph Smith asking for permission to establish a stake of the Church in Wisconsin.

A short time after this correspondence between Strang and Joseph Smith, the Prophet and his brother, Hyrum, were killed in Carthage, Illinois. Strang claimed that he had received a letter from Joseph Smith wherein Joseph had named Strang to be his successor—an interesting claim considering Strang had only been a member of the Church for a few months, had not received any temple ordinances, and had never served in a leadership position within the Church. Brigham Young called the letter a "wicked forgery." The letter is still in existence, and a few historians have taken sides as to its authenticity. Two of Strang's biographers wrote, "All seem to agree the signature bears no resemblance to that of [Joseph] Smith. All agree the letter was handprinted (not handwritten) by someone other than the Prophet."[8] Modern analysts agree that at least part of the letter is a forgery.

Strang did not go to Nauvoo to stake his claim as the new leader of the Church, but he did attend a conference of elders in Michigan and presented his case to them and showed them the letter he was supposed to have received from Joseph Smith. Because he was questioned so often as to whether he was or wasn't ordained to be the new prophet, Strang later began to tell people that on the very day that Joseph and Hyrum died, an angel came to him and anointed him to take Joseph's place as leader of The Church of Jesus Christ of Latter-day Saints.

Crandall Dunn, the presiding elder of the conference in Michigan, saw flaws in Strang's reasoning and did not believe the letter to be genuine. After further questioning and discovering that Strang had no license from the Church to preach, Crandall Dunn excommunicated Strang and sent a report of that action to the Quorum of the Twelve in Nauvoo. After the Twelve received word of the action taken against Strang, they validated Dunn's decision with an official excommunication.

Strang must have been charismatic because he continued to gain a following, and at one point was the most serious challenger to Brigham Young for Church leadership. He eventually obtained about two thousand followers, including former LDS Church leaders John E. Page, William Smith (Joseph's only surviving brother), William E. McLellin, John C. Bennet, and William E. Marks—not exactly the cream of the crop of former LDS church leaders, but former leaders nonetheless. Strang was ordained president of his church under the hands of William Smith and John C. Bennett, both of whom had been excommunicated in Nauvoo.

At first Strang had his members gather at Voree, Wisconsin. He even sent a letter to Nauvoo summoning the Twelve to Voree. When they did not show up, he excommunicated them. Later, he claimed that it had been revealed to him that Beaver Island in Lake Michigan was to be the gathering place of the Saints. Strang arrived on Beaver Island in 1847, and other Strangites settled there over the next few years. Strang claimed to receive revelations, and he even asserted that he had found and translated ancient metal plates. On July 9, 1850, James J. Strang had himself crowned "King of Beaver Island."

His desire to become a king will not be surprising to anyone who has studied his life or read his diary. On his nineteenth birthday, he wrote: "I am 19 years old and am yet no more than a common farmer. 'Tis too bad. I ought to have been a member of Assembly or a Brigadier General before this time if I am ever to rival Caesar or Napoleon which I have sworn to."[9] Several months later he wrote, "I have spent the day in trying to contrive some plan of obtaining in marriage the heir to the English Crown. It is a difficult business for me, but I shall try if there is the least chance. My mind has always been filled with dreams of royalty and power."[10]

James J. Strang created a church organization which consisted of himself as king, three viceroys, eight privy counselors, twelve cardinals, as well as princes, marquises, earls, chancellors, and knights. There developed serious problems within his church which ultimately led to Strang being shot and mortally wounded by two disaffected members of his church. Strang died July 9, 1856.[11]

The desire for wealth, power, and fame are powerful failings within mankind in his fallen and temporal condition. Some have turned to religion in order to fulfill this craving of the natural man. Elder Bruce R. McConkie wrote, "Apostasy is born of priestcrafts, for those who engage in them follow vain things, teach false doctrine, *love riches, and aspire to personal honors.*"[12]

NOTES

1. Lorenzo Snow, in *Collected Discourses*, vol. 1, 91.
2. Cited in Rich, *Little Known Schisms of the Restoration*, 23–24.
3. There were three "gift days" each year where members of Thompson's church were to give him special gifts: August 29, December 27, and, interestingly enough, April 15, which somehow seems appropriate.
4. Letter from Joseph F. Smith to George Q. Cannon, as cited in Britsch, *Unto the Islands of the Sea*, 123.
5. Ibid., 121.
6. Information on Walter Murray Gibson was taken from Gwynn Barrett, "Walter Murray Gibson: The Shepherd Saint of Lanai Revisited," *Utah Historical Quarterly*, vol. 40, no. 2, 142–62; Rich, *Those Who Would Be Leaders*, 52–56; Britsch, *Unto the Islands of the Sea*; and Shields, *Divergent Paths of the Restoration*, 85–86.
7. George A. Smith, in *Journal of Discourses*, 7:116.
8. Cronyn and Kenny, "The Saga of Beaver Island," in Fitzpatrick, *The King Strang Story*, 270.
9. *The Diary of James J. Strang*, 17.
10. Ibid., 19.
11. Information about James J. Strang was taken from Strang, *The Diary of James J. Strang*; Fitzpatrick, *The King Strang Story*; Rich, *Those Who Would Be Leaders*, 20–27; and Shields, *Divergent Paths of the Restoration*. There are still some Strangites in existence today. A 1975 source states that there were small groups at that time in Michigan, Wisconsin, Colorado, and New Mexico. Population estimates of Strang's church today vary between fifty to three hundred.
12. McConkie, *Mormon Doctrine*, 593, (emphasis added).

9

Being Deceived: Receiving or Believing False Revelation

Sometimes a person succumbs to apostasy simply because he has been deceived. Satan is the great deceiver and is capable of mixing in some truths in order to convince people of his lies. John Taylor remarked, "It is not every revelation that is of God, for Satan . . . can give visions and revelations as well as spiritual manifestations."[1] In scripture and in Church history we can read of the devil's attempts to appear as an angel of light that he might deceive those who are trying to follow God.

Of Satan's appearance to Moses found in the Pearl of Great Price, Orson Pratt wrote that "Satan came up before Moses, not in all his ugliness and maliciousness, but assuming the form of an angel of light."[2] Joseph Smith noted a time when he heard the voice of Adam the Archangel "detecting the devil when he appeared as an angel of light" (D&C 128:20).

Satan is a master of deception and convincing arguments, and a being of some, albeit limited, power. Through the use of his "signs and wonders" he has been able to deceive many. Elder Boyd K. Packer wrote:

> Be ever on guard lest you be deceived by inspiration from an unworthy source. You can be given false spiritual messages. There are counterfeit spirits just as there are counterfeit angels. (See Moroni 7:17.) Be careful lest you be deceived, for the devil may come disguised as an angel of light.

> The spiritual part of us and the emotional part of us are so closely linked that [it] is possible to mistake an emotional impulse for something spiritual. We occasionally find people who receive what they assume to be spiritual promptings from God, when those promptings are either centered in the emotions or are from the adversary.
>
> Avoid like a plague those who claim that some great spiritual experience authorizes them to challenge the constituted priesthood authority in the Church. Do not be unsettled if you cannot explain every insinuation of the apostate or every challenge from the enemies who attack the Lord's church. And we now face a tidal wave of that. In due time you will be able to confound the wicked and inspire the honest in heart.[3]

An individual does not have to personally receive false revelation or have actual contact with an evil spirit to be deceived. Many are deceived and fall into apostasy because they believe in others' false claims of revelation. Speaking of our dispensation, the Savior said, "For in those days there shall also arise false Christs, and false prophets, and shall show great signs and wonders, insomuch, that, if possible, they shall deceive the very elect" (JS—Matthew 1:22).

Unfortunately, over the years it has not been a few isolated incidents or extremely rare occurrences for Church members to have been deceived by false revelations. The Brethren have always been concerned about the possibility of the Saints being deceived and have addressed the subject in general conferences and have issued warnings from time to time.

In 1842 Joseph Smith wrote a lengthy editorial for the *Times and Seasons* entitled "Try the Spirits." The Prophet gave examples of people being deceived by false spirits anciently as recorded in the Old Testament and reported on some contemporary incidents with which he was familiar. He wrote that The Church of Jesus Christ of Latter-day Saints had experienced its share of false spirits. Joseph noted that "spirits of all kinds have been manifested, in every age and almost amongst all people";[4] and that "it is not to be wondered at if there should be found amongst us false spirits."[5] "We have also had," Joseph added, "brethren and sisters that have had written revelations, and have started forward to lead this church."[6] Joseph Smith was well aware of the reality of false revelation and the dangerous situation people faced if they were deceived by the adversary.

In 1913 the First Presidency of the Church issued "A Warning Voice," cautioning Latter-day Saints to be careful of listening to and following directions from the adversary. The entire statement was reissued by another First Presidency in the December 29, 1945, Church section of the *Deseret News*. Then, in 1970, Harold B. Lee reiterated "A Warning Voice" from the pulpit in general conference. Because of its importance to Church members then and now, the text of the original "A Warning Voice" has been included below in its entirety:

A WARNING VOICE

To the Officers and Members of The Church of Jesus Christ of Latter-day Saints:

From the days of Hiram Page (Doc. and Cov., Sec. 28), at different periods there have been manifestations from delusive spirits to members of the Church. Sometimes these have come to men and women who because of transgression became easy prey to the Arch-Deceiver. At other times people who pride themselves on their strict observance of the rules and ordinances and ceremonies of the Church are led astray by false spirits, who exercise an influence so imitative of that which proceeds from a Divine source that even these persons, who think they are "the very elect," find it difficult to discern the essential difference. Satan himself has transformed himself to be apparently "an angel of light."

When visions, dreams, tongues, prophecy, impressions or any extraordinary gift or inspiration conveys something out of harmony with the accepted revelations of the Church or contrary to the decisions of its constituted authorities, Latter-day Saints may know that it is not of God, no matter how plausible it may appear. Also they should understand that directions for the guidance of the Church will come, by revelation, through the head. All faithful members are entitled to the inspiration of the Holy Spirit for themselves, their families, and for those over whom they are appointed and ordained to preside. But anything at discord with that which comes from God through the head of the Church is not to be received as authoritative or reliable. In secular as well as spiritual affairs, Saints may receive Divine guidance and revelation affecting themselves, but this does not convey authority to direct others, and is not to be accepted when contrary to Church covenants, doctrine or discipline, or to known facts, demonstrated truths, or good common sense. No person has the right to induce his fellow members of the Church to engage in speculations or take stock in ventures of any kind on the specious claim of Divine revelation or vision or dream, especially when it is in opposition to the voice of recognized authority, local or general. The Lord's Church "is a house of order." It is not governed by individual gifts or manifestations, but by the order and power of the Holy Priesthood as sustained by the voice and vote of the Church in its appointed conferences.

The history of the Church records many pretended revelations claimed by impostors or zealots who believed in the manifestations they sought to lead other persons to accept, and in every instance, disappointment, sorrow and disaster have resulted therefrom. Financial loss and sometimes utter ruin have followed. We feel it our duty to warn the Latter-day Saints against fake mining schemes which have no warrant for success beyond the professed spiritual manifestations of their projectors and the influence gained over the excited minds of their victims. We caution the Saints against investing money or property in shares of stock which bring no profit to anyone but those who issue and trade in them. Fanciful schemes to make money for the alleged purpose of "redeeming Zion" or providing means for "the salvation of the dead" or other seemingly worthy objects, should not deceive anyone acquainted with the order of the Church, and will result only in waste of time and labor, which might be devoted now to doing something tangible and worthy and of record on earth and in heaven.

Be not led by any spirit or influence that discredits established authority, contradicts true scientific principles and discoveries, or leads away from the direct revelations of God for the government of the Church. The Holy Ghost does not contradict its own revealings. Truth is always harmonious with itself. Piety is often the cloak of error. The counsels of the Lord through the channel he has

> appointed will be followed with safety. Therefore, O! ye Latter-day Saints, profit by these words of warning.
>
> Joseph F. Smith, Anthon H. Lund, Charles W. Penrose,
> First Presidency[7]

In a 1970 priesthood session of general conference, President Harold B. Lee said, "It never ceases to amaze me how gullible some of our Church members are in broadcasting sensational stories, or dreams, or visions, or purported patriarchal blessings, or quotations, or supposedly from some person's private diary."[8] It may not be a huge number of Latter-day Saints that are deceived by false doctrines and false revelations, but if there are any deceived, it is too many.

The question arises, "Why and how are any Latter-day Saints deceived and led away from the plain truths of the gospel of Jesus Christ?" Let me suggest a possible explanation: Our Church had a remarkable, sensational beginning which included visions and visits from angels, the Savior, and even God the Father. Those who have joined with the Latter-day Saints believe and have faith in these supernal spiritual experiences. Add to that belief the doctrine that every worthy member can and should receive personal revelation. Remember, it was the Prophet Joseph who said, "God hath not revealed anything to Joseph, but what He will make known unto the Twelve, and even the least Saint may know all things as fast as he is able to bear them."[9]

We believe that God speaks to His children. We believe in answers to prayers and spiritual guidance. However, we also know that the adversary is capable of sending false spiritual messages. The problem arises when individuals receive what they believe is revelation from God, but they have either been deceived by the adversary or by their own emotions. The possibility of being influenced and deceived by the wrong source becomes more probable if a person is not grounded in true doctrine and not familiar with the workings of the true Spirit.

Because we do believe in a spiritual realm and in receiving personal revelation, it becomes more apparent how some members of our Church could be swayed either by their own personal experiences or by sensational experiences of others if they believe those experiences to have come from God. The key is to not lose our faith in communication from heaven, but at the same time always being vigilant so that we are not deceived by communication from the wrong source. The Lord wants us to be a believing people, but He does not want us to be a gullible people. The Prophet Joseph Smith said that "nothing is a greater injury to the children of men than to be under the influence of a false spirit when they think they have the Spirit of God."[10]

Why do we lose people to individual apostasy and apostate groups? In many cases it is because they have been confused by their emotions, or by information from a false source, or by accounts of supernatural experiences shared by would-be prophets. Either they do not understand true doctrine or else they are blinded by their pride to the fact that God will work solely through the living prophet when sending revelation for the Church.

Elder Boyd K. Packer gave some wise council to the youth of the Church in 1994: "Now, young people, pay attention! Before I say another word about personal revelation, I must tell you so that you cannot possibly misunderstand: 'There are many spirits which are false spirits' (D&C 50:2). There can be counterfeit revelations, promptings from the devil, temptations! As long as you live, in one way or another the adversary will try to lead you astray."[11]

In 1958 nine missionaries, six elders and three sisters, were excommunicated for apostasy while serving missions in France. Seven of them never came back to the Church, but got involved with an LDS break-off organization called the Church of the Firstborn of the Fulness of Times.

Although all nine were involved to a greater or lesser degree in the apostasy, it appears that one elder in particular was the driving force behind most of the problems. He was charismatic, outspoken, and quite knowledgeable. But he was also subversive, secretive, and lived a double life. His discussions with fellow missionaries confused them and caused doubt. He preached false doctrine and deceived those who were not doctrinally sound. Yet after only a few years involvement with his new church, he also abandoned them and died an avowed atheist.[12] What will be his fate as he stands before the judgment bar of God?

There seems to be a great difference between those who have been deceived and those who are deceivers. Only God can judge the hearts of people, and so we are left to wonder what will happen to people like the apostate missionary in France, William Law, Walter Murray Gibson, and James J. Strang. Were they deceived by Satan and sincerely believed that they were doing God's will? Or were they completely aware that they were deceiving and exploiting their followers?

Korihor was an anti-Christ who confronted the prophet Alma in the Book of Mormon. We read that Korihor led "away the hearts of many, causing them to lift up their heads in their wickedness" (Alma 30:18). When he is later shown a sign of the power of God in which he is struck dumb, Korihor writes, "The devil hath deceived me; for he appeared unto me in the form of an angel, and said unto me: Go and reclaim this people, for they have all gone astray after an unknown God" (Alma 30:53).

Was Korihor an innocent pawn in the hands of the great deceiver? Did he actually believe that what he was doing was right? Or did he knowingly enlist with the adversary in his game of deceit? Korihor also wrote that the devil told him that there was no God and taught him what to say; and "I have taught his words . . . because they were pleasing unto the carnal mind; and I taught them, even until I had much success, insomuch that I verily believed that they were true" (Alma 30:53). Korihor said that he was deceived by Satan, yet he also wrote, "I always knew that there was a God" (Alma 30:52). Not knowing the whole story or his heart, it would be impossible for man to know how to judge Korihor.

I have become acquainted with people who belong to break-off churches from The Church of Jesus Christ of Latter-day Saints. Most of the people I have met are good, decent individuals who believe in God and in the restoration of the gospel through the Prophet Joseph Smith. They are doing what they believe is right and are trying their best to follow the Savior. I have been greatly concerned about what will happen to them in the life to come. While pondering these things I came upon the following verses from the Doctrine and Covenants: "But wo unto them that are deceivers and hypocrites, for, thus saith the Lord, I will bring them to judgment." The consequences of being a deceiver sound dire. But the next verse gave me peace and hope for those who have been deceived. "Behold, verily I say unto you, there are hypocrites among you, who have deceived some, which has given the adversary power; but behold such shall be reclaimed" (D&C 50:6–7).

Judgment will come upon all mankind. The hypocrites and deceivers will have to stand before God and answer for the damage they have done. However, of the "some" referred to who have been deceived, it appears that through the Atonement of Christ they can be reclaimed. Elder Orson F. Whitney gave these comforting words to any of us who may have temporarily lost loved ones to the wiles of the adversary:

> Though some of the sheep may wander, the eye of the Shepherd is upon them, and sooner or later they will feel the tentacles of Divine Providence reaching out after them and drawing them back to the fold. Either in this life or the life to come, they will return. They will have to pay their debt to justice; they will suffer for their sins; and may tread a thorny path; but if it leads them at last, like the penitent Prodigal, to a loving and forgiving father's heart and home, the painful experience will not have been in vain. Pray for your careless and disobedient children; hold on to them with your faith. Hope on, trust on, till you see the salvation of God.[13]

There are some basic principles to follow in order to protect ourselves from being deceived. First, "whoso treasureth up my word, shall not be deceived" (JS—Matthew 1:37). God's word is found in the standard works, the teachings of the prophets, and in the whisperings of the Holy Ghost. If a person receives what they believe to be a revelation through the Spirit, but it does not match what is being taught by living prophets or found in the standard works, that person has tapped into a source other than God.[14]

Second, be careful not to misunderstand or misinterpret spiritual manifestations, your own or those related to you by others. Our personal spiritual experiences are meant to remain private unless we are otherwise moved upon by the Spirit. Even then, we must remember that unique spiritual occurrences do not define the doctrine of the Church.

As an example, a married couple loses a young child to death and are going through a very difficult time of grieving. The little girl who had passed away comes to one of the parents in a dream, happy and smiling. This experience brings great comfort and peace to the grieving couple, but some might interpret the incident as revealing a doctrine that there are little children spirits in the spirit world. President Joseph F. Smith taught that spirits "possessed their full stature in the spirit, before they entered mortality, the same stature that they will possess after they have passed away from mortality."[15]

In this situation, a prophet of God has already established the doctrine of the Church. The purpose of the dream was to bring comfort to the couple, not to teach a doctrine. Elder M. Russell Ballard said, "I must point out that individual spiritual experiences of Church members do not determine Church doctrine."[16]

Third, do not follow those who "set themselves up for a light unto the world, that they may get gain and praise of the world" (2 Nephi 26:29). There have been those who claim to be recipients of unusual spiritual manifestations and believe this gives them the responsibility to direct the lives of others. This sometimes puts them in opposition to the official teachings of the Church.

After my mission I was attending a young single adult ward at a university. In priesthood meeting a young man told the quorum that he had died, gone beyond the veil, and returned from the spirit world. The story was amazing, and I was impressed the first time I heard it. After I heard him share the same account week after week in priesthood meeting and Sunday school, however, I felt a little troubled each time he raised his hand. One day the teacher quoted a statement by the Prophet Joseph Smith to which this young man responded, "Well, that's not true. I have been beyond the veil and have seen the way things really are." Flashing warning lights should have gone off in the mind of every person in that room.

I'm not sure whether this young man had really been beyond the veil or not, although I was more than suspicious when he disagreed with doctrine taught by Joseph Smith. But even if his experience was genuine, it would have been for his personal understanding and NOT for the dispensing of doctrine. Boyd K. Packer said, "An unusual spiritual experience should not be regarded as a personal call to direct others. It is my conviction that experiences of a special, sacred nature are individual and should be kept to oneself."[17]

It becomes much worse when someone has been deceived by the adversary and is persuading others to follow him. As Church members we should be wary of the fantastic, unnecessary revelations that come from questionable sources. Beware of those who share fantastic stories that do not ring true. For example, why would a hitchhiker who tells the people who picked him up to get their food storage ready and then disappears from the back seat of their car even be needed when apostles and prophets give us that message at general conference? Why should Church members be more apt to act upon the rumored dreams and visions of fringe members of the Church than they are the counsel of a living prophet? God does not send revelations for the Church through anyone but the living prophet.

I get very concerned when I hear of Latter-day Saints actually being deceived by people with tales of secret priesthood ordinations, caves containing revelations translated by the one "mighty and strong" because our Church leaders could not translate them, ordinances of a more sacred nature than performed in our temples, secret scripture codes with warnings only meant to be understood by the spiritual elite, and amazing patriarchal blessings shared in a Sunday School class by someone who "knows it is true" because the blessing was given to his missionary companion's friend's cousin's neighbor.

If we are not careful, we will find ourselves "tossed to and fro, and carried about with every wind of doctrine, by the sleight of men, and cunning craftiness, whereby they lie in wait to deceive" (Ephesians 4:14). "Few things disturb the channels of revelation quite so effectively," said Elder Packer, "as those who are misled and think themselves to be chosen to instruct others when they are not chosen."[18] The admonition given by the Lord in 1831 is just as valid today: "Beware lest ye are deceived" (D&C 46:8).

NOTES

1. John Taylor, in *Latter-day Prophets Speak*, 22.
2. Orson Pratt, in *Journal of Discourses*, 15:235.
3. Boyd K. Packer, "The Candle of the Lord," *Ensign*, January 1983, 55–56.
4. Joseph Smith, "Try the Spirits," *Times and Seasons*, vol. 3, 743.
5. Ibid., 747.
6. Ibid.
7. *Messages of the First Presidency*, 4:285–86.
8. Harold B. Lee, "To the Defenders of the Faith," *Improvement Era*, June 1970, 64.
9. Smith, *Teachings of the Prophet Joseph Smith*, 149.
10. Ibid., 205.
11. Boyd K. Packer, "Personal Revelation: The Gift, the Test, and the Promise," *Ensign*, Nov. 1994, 61.
12. Kahlile Mehr, "The Trial of the French Mission," *Dialogue*, vol. 21, no. 3, Fall 1988.
13. Orson F. Whitney, *Conference Report*, Apr. 1929, 110.
14. Let me suggest an analogy from mathematics to help us determine true doctrine. Take any given point and there are an infinite number of straight lines that can pass through that point. However, if there are two points, only one straight line can pass through those two points. Similarly, if we can align a doctrine taught in the standard works and by the living prophets we have true doctrine. Add the third point of confirmation by the Spirit and it is even better. We should be careful not to base our belief in a particular doctrine on one point only. A scripture can be misinterpreted. We can be deceived by a false spirit. We might misunderstand what has been taught by one of the Brethren, or he might have simply expressed an opinion. But if we can align two or three of these "points" we will be safe from deception.
15. Smith, *Gospel Doctrine*, 445. Joseph F. Smith said that he learned this from his father, the Patriarch Hyrum Smith. President Smith also stated, "If you see one of your children that has passed away it may appear to you in the form in which you would recognize it, the form of childhood; but if it came to you as a messenger bearing some important truth, it would perhaps come . . . in the stature of full-grown manhood." Ibid.

16. M. Russell Ballard, "Suicide: Some Things We Know, and Some Things We Do Not," *Ensign*, Oct. 1987, 8.
17. Boyd K. Packer, "Revelation in a Changing World," *Ensign*, Nov. 1989, 15.
18. Ibid.

10

How to Avoid Apostasy

We are the Saints of the latter days, living in the dispensation of the fulness of times. The Lord has promised us that His Church will never again be taken from the earth. There will not be another great apostasy. But, as we have learned, personal apostasy will happen and will increase in frequency until the Second Coming of Jesus Christ. We must be ever alert to the dangers of personal apostasy and the heartbreaking consequences it can bring.

George Q. Cannon stated that apostasy was to be dreaded by members of the Church. President Cannon said:

> I cannot think of anything that would fill me with deeper sorrow, next to the loss of my own salvation, than the thought that my name would be blotted out, that my descendants would be blotted out, and I would not have a man of my descent throughout the Millennium to stand before the Lord bearing the Priesthood. God forbid that such a fate should happen to any of us, especially those who have been faithful in the Church of Christ! Therefore, *apostasy ought to be dreaded, and the dread of it ought to be instilled into every heart,* and into the heart of every child, so that it will grow up loving the truth, loving the Church, hating iniquity, clinging to that which is virtuous and pure and that which will preserve the Spirit of God.[1]

In these last days prior to Jesus returning to the earth to usher in the Millennium, the adversary is doing everything he can to "deceive the very elect" (JS—Matthew 1:22). Elder Carlos E. Asay wrote of the barrage of anti-Mormonism we have faced since the earliest days of the restoration: "Since the spring of 1820, Lucifer has led a relentless attack against the Latter-day Saints and their leaders. A parade of anti-Christs, anti-Mormons, and apostate groups have appeared on the scene. Many are still among us and have released new floods of lies and false accusations. These faith-killers and testimony-thieves use personal contacts, the printed word, electronic media, and other means of communication to sow doubts and disturb the peace of true believers."[2]

Each of us is likely familiar with an "elect person" who has been deceived. People who had at one time been very strong in their testimonies and determination to serve God have fallen away. It is frightening to think that every one of us is capable of being deceived if we do not make the efforts necessary to keep us on the strait and narrow.

Knowing that the seeds of apostasy are within each of us, and that absolutely everyone is subject to being deceived and wandering away from the path, what can we do to insure that we do not fall? How can we avoid being deceived?

The answers are so basic that they might be referred to as the "Sunday School answers." Regardless of their simplicity, these fundamental principles of the gospel are effective. Prayer, scripture study, learning the doctrine, obeying commandments, keeping covenants, and service in the kingdom of God will keep us safe. When applied correctly and sincerely, so-called Sunday school answers really do work.

The following are principles that, if followed, can help us protect ourselves and our families from straying from the straight and narrow path onto strange roads and forbidden paths.

Pray Daily

Daily communication with our Father in Heaven through prayer and personal revelation is absolutely necessary to become and keep ourselves strong in the faith. Remember President Brigham Young's statement that he prayed to God every day to preserve him from falling away.[3] Elder Boyd K. Packer of the Quorum of the Twelve declared,

"No one of us can survive in the world of today, much less in what it soon will become, without personal inspiration."[4]

Elder Packer also said, "Prayer is so essential a part of revelation that without it the veil may remain closed to you. Learn to pray. Pray often. Pray in your mind, in your heart. Pray on your knees."[5] President Spencer W. Kimball stated that members of the Church who are wise will avoid even taking the first step toward apostasy by praying "frequently and regularly."[6] President Kimball also suggested that we pray for Church leaders and that if children are taught to pray for the leaders of the Church "they are quite unlikely to ever fall into apostasy."[7]

President George Q. Cannon spoke out on the efficacy of prayer in distancing oneself from the very serious sin of apostasy:

> Apostasy is a dreadful crime. No matter who it is that apostatizes from the truth, breaks the commandments of God, violates the covenants that he or she has made with the Almighty and denies the faith, it is a dreadful crime. It cannot be glossed over; it cannot be made light of; it is a serious offense, upon which God has set the seal of His condemnation. Children should be taught this in their early life. The mother, when she gathers her children around her knee and teaches them to pray, should teach them to pray that they may be preserved in the truth, that they may be kept from sin, that they may be enabled to maintain the faith.[8]

Study the Scriptures

There are so many aspects of scripture study that are essential in our quest to stay on the path that leads to eternal life. Our questions, problems, and prayers will often be answered by passages of scripture. Scripture study opens the door to personal revelation. Daily scripture study helps us maintain the Holy Ghost as a constant companion and strengthens our resistance to temptation. Scripture study is also for the learning of doctrine; and the best defense against false doctrine is true doctrine.

Harold B. Lee admonished Church members to study the scriptures every day. "Do you have a daily habit of reading the scriptures? If we're not reading the scriptures daily, our testimonies are growing thinner, our spirituality isn't increasing in depth."[9]

Spencer W. Kimball bore a strong personal witness about the importance of scripture study in his life. He said: "I find that when I get casual in my relationships with divinity and when it seems that no divine ear is listening and no divine voice is speaking, that I am far, far away. If I immerse myself in the scriptures the distance narrows and the spirituality returns. I find myself loving more intensely those whom I must love with all my heart and mind and strength, and loving them more, I find it easier to abide their counsel."[10]

Will daily scripture study actually protect us from falling away from the faith? Yes! Remember the promise the Lord made to those of the last days: "And whoso treasureth up my word, shall not be deceived" (JS—Matthew 1:37).

Learn the Doctrine

Brigham Young taught that "we will never cease to learn, unless we apostatize from the religion of Jesus Christ."[11] We hear doctrine taught in our meetings each week, in our family home evenings, in classrooms, and from the pulpit. How can we be sure that the doctrine being taught is correct?

As previously mentioned, the best defense against false doctrine is an understanding of true doctrine. President Joseph F. Smith said that false doctrine within the Church usually comes from one of two sources: people too lazy to study and arrogant individuals who think they know everything there is to know about the gospel. "Beware of the lazy and the proud," warned President Smith.[12]

Consistent gospel study protects us from being deceived by false doctrine because it increases our knowledge and helps us understand true doctrines more clearly. "How do these false teachers lead people astray?" asked Elder Mark E. Peterson. "They do so by attacking the fundamental doctrines of the Church. . . . They seek to develop doctrinal disputes among the people to undermine their faith, and they lead people to apostasy when they do such things as that."[13]

How many Church members over the years could have been spared the mistaken wanderings on paths of apostasy had they truly understood the doctrines of the kingdom of God? Elder Joseph B. Wirthlin taught that "faithful members of the Church should be like oak trees and should extend deep roots into the fertile soil of the fundamental principles of the gospel." He said that by understanding and living the basic gospel truths we would be able to "withstand the winds of temptation, false doctrine, adversity, and the onslaught of the adversary without being swayed or uprooted."[14]

Each person should strive to become a gospel scholar. Parents need to teach their children the plain and precious doctrines of the kingdom, beginning when the children are very young, and continue the process throughout their young lives. Imagine missionaries entering their fields of labor with a solid doctrinal foundation learned in the home.

Young men and women of the Church who are taught the gospel by loving parents, and who are instructed and encouraged to study the scriptures daily, have a greater degree of protection against the adversary. Harold B. Lee commented that, historically, those who have apostatized from the Church did so "for one of two reasons—either because they have sinned and lost the faith, or they're ignorant of the doctrines of the Church." He concluded that "if we, as the Church, expect the family can be ignorant and safe, we expect what never was and never will be."[15]

Obey the Commandments

We've seen how unrepented serious transgression can result in apostasy. Disobedience leads us away from God, which leads us away from happiness. Transgression alters our thinking and blinds us to light and truth. When Adam and Eve were in the Garden of Eden they enjoyed a personal association with God the Father. President Marion G. Romney taught that Heavenly Father "visited them in the Garden of Eden and conversed with and instructed them."[16]

After Adam and Eve transgressed, they actually hid from God. The Father called unto Adam saying, "Where goest thou?" (Moses 4:15). BYU religion professor Alonzo Gaskill wrote that this was "a rhetorical question asked by God, designed to provoke in Adam introspection regarding the path being pursued."[17] In other words, "Adam, look at the direction you are going. Are you moving toward God or away from

God? Why would you move away from a loving Father who only wants what is best for you?" When we transgress the laws of God we often do not see things clearly and may actually flee from or fight against the very thing that can bring us true happiness and peace.

Obedience to God's laws brings the Spirit into our lives, which makes it possible for us to see things as they really are. "He that keepeth his commandments receiveth truth and light, until he is glorified in truth and knoweth all things" (D&C 93:28). "And that wicked one cometh and taketh away light and truth, through disobedience" (D&C 93:39).

Joseph Smith taught the importance of keeping the commandments to keep oneself safe from apostasy. One man wrote that he went with his mother to Nauvoo and heard the Prophet Joseph preach his last sermon. Joseph "told the people what to do to avoid apostasy. He stood in the pulpit and then said 'Attend to your prayers, pay an honest tithing, obey the authorities and follow the records of this Church and you will never apostatize.' "[18]

George Q. Cannon asked the question, "When will apostasy cease?" Answering his own question he remarked, "It is sin that causes apostasy. No man ever apostatized from this Church who had not committed sin. God does not desert those who are faithful and keep His commandments."[19]

Keep the Covenants

Closely related to keeping the commandments of God is faithful observance of the covenants we have made at baptism, relating to receiving the priesthood, and the sacred covenants made in the temple. Modern dictionaries define a covenant as an agreement or contract between two parties. Subsequent definitions refer to conditional promises made by God to man. The gospel covenants we make are between us and our Father in Heaven.

God does not break covenants, so if a covenant is broken it is always broken by man. I once heard a story about a married couple who were driving home one night after attending a social event. They drove in silence for a little while until the wife said, "Remember when we were dating and after we were first married—how we always sat close to each other, even when we were in the car?" There was a hint of sadness in her voice. The husband thought for a moment and replied, "I haven't moved." In like manner, if we are not as close to God as we once were, we can be assured that it is not God who moved. When we break covenants we are moving away from our Father in Heaven.

Breaking covenants that we have made with God can result in us quickly losing the Spirit. Spencer W. Kimball said that we need to attend our sacrament meetings each week so that we would remember the covenants we have made. He continued:

> When you look in the dictionary for the most important word, do you know what it is? It could be *remember.* Because all of you have made covenants—you know what to do and you know how to do it—our greatest need is to remember. That is why everyone goes to sacrament meeting every Sabbath day—to take the sacrament and listen to the priests pray that they "may always remember him and keep his commandments which he has given them." Nobody should ever forget to go to sacrament meeting. *Remember* is the word. *Remember* is the program.[20]

President Kimball also wrote, "I suppose there would never be an apostate, there would never be a crime, if people remembered, really remembered, the things they had covenanted at the water's edge or at the sacrament table and in the temple."[21] Clearly, regular attendance at sacrament meetings can help us remember and keep our covenants.

Elder Melvin J. Ballard noted that apostasy is a slow process, and that no one "goes away from this Church and becomes an apostate in a week, nor in a month." He then commented on the importance of partaking of the sacrament each week: "The one thing that would make for the safety of every man and woman would be to appear at the sacrament table every Sabbath day. We would not get very far away in one week—not so far that, by the process of self-investigation, we could not rectify the wrongs we may have done."[22]

Serve in the Kingdom of God

Jesus told His disciples that among the Gentiles there were leaders who exercised lordship over other Gentiles; "and their great ones exercise authority upon them. But so shall it not be among you: but whosever will be great among you, shall be your minister: And whosoever of you will be the chiefest, shall be servant of all" (Mark 10:42–44). Service to others is one of the most important aspects of the kingdom of God. Even Church leaders are in reality the servants of the members of the Church.

It is not position or calling in the Church, but rather one's willingness to serve others that is one of the most important signs of being valiant in the kingdom. Hugh Nibley shared the following personal insight:

> I have always been furiously active in the Church, but I have . . . never held any office of rank in anything. I have undertaken many assignments given me by the leaders, and much of the work has been anonymous: no rank, no recognition, no anything. While I have been commended for some things, they were never the things which I considered most important. That was entirely a little understanding between me and my Heavenly Father which I have thoroughly enjoyed, though no one else knows anything about it. . . . *I would rather be a doorkeeper in the House of the Lord than mingle with the top brass in the tents of the wicked.*[23]

From an article in the May 1901 Church magazine the *Improvement Era* comes this statement: "Pride of office should have no place in the Church of Christ, and only he who is willing to serve in the humblest capacity is worthy to be placed in positions of trust."[24] Harold B. Lee said, "We have men who are willing to give their lives, give all they possess in service and devotion . . . and then we have those who are on the outer fringes, who hardly know whether they are members of the Church or not—almost to the point of complete apostasy."[25]

From the scriptures we "learn that when ye are in the service of your fellow beings ye are only in the service of your God" (Mosiah 2:17). We demonstrate our love for God and for His children, our brothers and sisters, through selfless service. This type of Christlike love "includes kindness, tenderness, understanding, mercy, forgiveness, affection, and ultimately a willingness to sacrifice all that one has, if necessary. The absence of love is a sign of apostasy."[26]

Our love for and desire to serve others can be demonstrated in our willingness to spend our time, efforts, skills, and in giving financial help to those in need. Elder Russell M. Nelson said, "At least once a month, we fast and pray and contribute generous offerings to funds that enable bishops to disperse aid. This is part of the law of the gospel. Each of us truly can help the poor and the needy, now, and wherever they are. *And we, too, will be blessed and protected from apostasy by so doing.*"[27]

Service also includes accepting and magnifying callings we may receive in the various quorums and auxiliaries of the Church. Neglecting the responsibilities of a Church calling is a sin of omission, and President Joseph Fielding Smith warned that "apostasy comes through the sins of omission as well as through sins of commission."[28] Wilford Woodruff said that "it is through this neglect of duty that so many have left this Church and kingdom of God."[29]

If we want our resolve to stay active in the Church to remain strong and our testimonies to grow, we must consistently be of service to our brothers and sisters, both inside and outside of the Church. "There is great security in spirituality," wrote President Spencer W. Kimball, "and we cannot have spirituality without service!"[30]

Follow the Brethren

Faithfulness in the Kingdom of God requires us to have faith in the servants of God. The apostle John wrote, "If a man say, I love God, and hateth his brother, he is a liar" (1 John 4:20). In like manner, a person who claims to love and follow the Savior is not truly a follower of the Lord if he refuses to follow those whom God has chosen to be His spokesmen, His apostles and prophets. The Lord said whether His instruction comes "by mine own voice or by the voice of my servants, it is the same" (D&C 1:38).

President Marion G. Romney said, "Some members assume that one can be in full harmony with the spirit of the gospel, enjoy full fellowship in the Church, and at the same time be out of harmony with the leaders of the Church and the counsel and direction they give." He stated that "such a position is wholly inconsistent, because the guidance of this Church comes not alone from the written word but also from continuous revelation, and the Lord gives that revelation to the Church through his chosen prophet." President Romney concluded that "those who profess to accept the gospel and who at the same time criticize and refuse to follow the counsel of the prophet are assuming an indefensible position. Such a spirit leads to apostasy. It is not new. It was prevalent in the days of Jesus and in the days of the Prophet Joseph Smith."[31]

Don't Be Troubled by Changes

The ninth Article of Faith reads: "We believe all that God has revealed, all that He does now reveal, and *we believe that He will yet reveal many great and important things pertaining to the Kingdom of God"* (emphasis added). It is important for us to remember that the Church will continue to grow and develop as further light and truth is revealed. We cannot become so "locked in" to the way things are that we are not willing to change when God expands our knowledge of truth through modern revelation. The Book of Mormon speaks of a time when people will not accept more of the revealed word of God with the cry of "A Bible! A Bible! We have got a Bible, and there cannot be any more Bible" (2 Nephi 29:3).

One of the most common complaints from modern apostates is that today's Church is not the same as it was in the days of Joseph Smith. This criticism is certainly not new. Within a few short years after the Church was organized, there were some people who did not like the organizational changes made or the new doctrines revealed through the Prophet Joseph Smith himself. Joseph was not hesitant to alter or add to Church doctrine under God's command. Almost every new change seems to have challenged the faith of some people in the Church.

Section 76 of the Doctrine and Covenants or the revelation known as "The Vision" was revealed to the Prophet Joseph and Sidney Rigdon in February 1832. Some Church members had difficulty accepting the newly revealed truth because it differed from the traditional views of life after death. Early Mormon missionary John Murdock recorded in his diary that a number of "the brethren had just received the Revilation [sic] called the vision and were stumbling at it."[32] Concerning the same revelation, Orson Pratt wrote in his journal that one high priest was still rejecting the Vision nearly two years after it was received, saying "it was of the devil."[33]

Elder Boyd K. Packer spoke of "those within the Church who are disturbed when changes are made with which they disagree or when changes they propose are not made." Elder Packer said that this type of people point to these changes as evidence that our Church leaders are not inspired. He noted that "they write and speak to convince others that the doctrines and decisions of the Brethren are not given through inspiration. Two things characterize them: they are always irritated by the word *obedience,* and always they question revelation. It has always been so."[34]

Former Latter-day Saints who have become critics of the Church have complained about changes in policies, additions received by prophets to the canon of our scriptures, and clarification of doctrine also received by living prophets. They pick and choose the doctrines and the prophets they will accept as if the gospel were some type of buffet or smorgasbord. I've read books by some who have left the Church to start their own religion. They will quote one of our latter day prophets if he appears to be supporting their views, and on the very next page reject the same Church president because he taught something in opposition to their chosen doctrine, calling him a fallen prophet.

Elder James E. Faust said that for some it seems easier "to believe the words of dead prophets rather than those of living prophets."[35] During His mortal ministry Jesus reproved the Jews who did not accept Him, saying that they garnished the sepulchers of the dead prophets while rejecting the living prophets.

Don't Be Offended

Most of us know people who have either become inactive or left the Church entirely because they were offended by someone or something in the Church. Sometimes people are offended because they are not keeping the commandments and when they hear a message of repentance they choose to be offended. After Nephi spoke to his rebellious brothers they accused him of declaring unto them hard things. Nephi responded that he knew he had "spoken hard things against the wicked, according to the truth; and the righteous have I justified, and testified that they should be lifted up at the last day; wherefore, the guilty taketh the truth to be hard, for it cutteth them to the very center" (1 Nephi 16:2).

There are those who have been offended by the insensitivity of ward members or leaders. Individuals or families will at times believe that they have been slighted in some way. The bishop did nothing to help their family in time of need. The Young Women leaders ignored the new girl who just moved into the ward. No one in the ward welcomed or spoke to the new convert the week after his baptism.

Whether these offenses were real or imagined, it is not the gospel of Jesus Christ but imperfect individuals within the Church that are the problem. In many cases it is the people who took offense that are causing the difficulty.

The following is an excerpt from Elder Bednar's classic October 2006 conference address entitled "And Nothing Shall Offend Them":

> When we believe or say we have been offended, we usually mean we feel insulted, mistreated, snubbed, or disrespected. And certainly clumsy, embarrassing, unprincipled, and mean-spirited things do occur in our interactions with other people that would allow us to take offense. However, it ultimately is impossible for another person to offend you or to offend me. Indeed, believing that another person offended us is fundamentally false. To be offended is a *choice* we make; it is not a *condition* inflicted or imposed upon us by someone or something else.[36]

We can use Brigham Young as an example of someone who could have left the Church, but was wise enough and humble enough to remain faithful. Brigham Young said that when the Vision first came to his attention, he struggled because it was contrary to what he had previously learned, but he told himself to wait a little and he did not reject it.[37] He did not let new revelations and changes cause him to lose faith.

Robert Horne related a story about Brigham Young's faith in the restored gospel and his determination not to become an apostate. The Prophet Joseph once said to a group of brethren that included Horne and Brigham Young, "If I were to tell you all I know of the kingdom of God, I do know that you would rise up and kill me." Horne recalled that Brigham Young arose at that moment and said, "Don't tell me anything that I can't bear, for I don't want to apostatize."[38]

There is an undocumented story passed down through Brigham Young's descendants recounting a time when Brigham received a public chastisement by the Prophet Joseph—what appeared to be "a deliberate and public blow to the very core of the man, his pride." According to the family legend, Brother Brigham arose and said, "Joseph, what do you want me to do?" Joseph wept and embraced Brigham and told him that he had passed the test.[39]

Whether the incident mentioned above actually happened or not, the principle is true. Whether an offense was accidental or on purpose, we choose whether or not to be offended. By deciding to be offended by someone or something connected to the Church, we risk losing the Spirit. There have been far too many Latter-day Saints who have become embittered and separated themselves from the true gospel of Jesus Christ because they allowed themselves to become offended.

Watch Yourself

Finally, one of the most important things we can do to avoid personal apostasy is to be consistent and honest in self-examination. We cannot rationalize our way out of faithful obedience or justify any disobedience to God's laws by thinking we are the exception to the rule. The scriptures tell us that we need to watch ourselves. "But this much I can tell you, that if ye do not watch yourselves, and your thoughts, and your words, and your deeds, and observe the commandments of God, and continue in the faith of what ye have heard concerning the coming of our Lord, even unto the end of your lives, ye must perish. And now, O man, remember, and perish not" (Mosiah 4:30).

When we sincerely examine our thoughts, words, actions, and even the motives for our actions, and strive to do the right things for the best reasons, we will continue along the path that leads to eternal happiness. Humble followers of the Savior do not become apostates. Being humble plays a major role in keeping us safe from apostasy.

NOTES

1. George Q. Cannon, in *Collected Discourses,* 4:395, emphasis added.
2. Carlos E. Asay, "Opposition to the Work of God," *Ensign,* November 1981, 67.
3. Brigham Young, in *Journal of Discourses,* 5:213.
4. Boyd K. Packer, "Reverence Invites Revelation" *Ensign,* Nov. 1991, 23.
5. Boyd K. Packer, "Personal Revelation: The Gift, the Test, and the Promise," *Ensign,* Nov. 1994, 59.
6. Kimball, *Miracle of Forgiveness,* 132.
7. Kimball, *Teachings of Spencer W. Kimball,* 121.
8. Cannon, *Gospel Truths,* 2:64.
9. Lee, *Teachings of Harold B. Lee,* 152.
10. Kimball, *Teachings of Spencer W. Kimball,* 135.
11. Brigham Young, in *Journal of Discourses,* 3:203.
12. Smith, *Gospel Doctrine,* 373.
13. Mark E. Peterson, "Be Ye Not Deceived . . . ," *Improvement Era,* November 1945, 655.
14. Joseph B. Wirthlin, "Deep Roots," *Ensign,* Nov. 1994, 75.
15. Lee, *Teachings of Harold B. Lee,* 298.
16. Marion G. Romney, "Easter Thoughts," *Ensign,* May 1975, 82.
17. Gaskill, *The Savior and the Serpent,* 77.
18. Found in McConkie, *Remembering Joseph* Companion CD-ROM under "Bunnell, Stephen Ithamar."
19. George Q. Cannon, in *Collected Discourses,* 4:344.
20. Spencer W. Kimball, "Circles of Exaltation," in *The Charge to Religious Educators,* 1st edition, 23.
21. Kimball, *Teachings of Spencer W. Kimball,* 112.
22. Melvin J. Ballard, "Sacramental Covenant," *Improvement Era,* Oct. 1919, 1028.
23. Nibley, *Old Testament and Related Studies,* vii, emphasis added. I also appreciate what Dr. Alonzo Gaskill shared with me about leadership and service. He said that he was struck with the fact that the leaders of our wards and stakes, and even more so the General Church leadership, do not "get served," but rather serve their hearts out. "The common myth that position equals privilege is exactly that—a myth! Being called to a position of leadership is

less of an honor, and more of a burden or responsibility. It is a calling to serve and sacrifice."

24. Attewall Wootton, "Humility With Power," *Improvement Era*, May 1901, 513.
25. Lee, *Teachings of Harold B. Lee*, 142–43.
26. Vivian Paulsen, "Love," *Encyclopedia of Mormonism*, 2:847.
27. Russell M. Nelson, "In the Lord's Own Way," *Ensign*, May 1986, 27, emphasis added.
28. Smith, *Church History and Modern Revelation*, 3:150.
29. Wilford Woodruff, in *Journal of Discourses*, 21:282.
30. Spencer W. Kimball, "Small Acts of Service," *Ensign*, Dec. 1974, 5.
31. Marion G. Romney, "Unity," *Ensign*, May 1983, 17.
32. John Murdock Diary as cited in Woodford, "The Historical Development of the Doctrine and Covenants," 929.
33. Pratt, *The Orson Pratt Journals*, 29.
34. Boyd K. Packer, "Revelation in a Changing World," *Ensign*, Nov. 1989, 15.
35. James E. Faust, "Continuous Revelation," *Ensign*, Nov. 1989, 9.
36. David A. Bednar, "And Nothing Shall Offend Them," *Ensign*, Nov. 2006, 90.
37. Brigham Young, in *Deseret News*, Sept. 14, 1852, as cited in Woodford, "The Historical Development of the Doctrine and Covenants," 929.
38. "Reminiscences of the Church in Nauvoo," *Millennial Star*, vol. 55, Sept. 4, 1893, 585.
39. Truman G. Madsen, "Hugh B. Brown—Youthful Veteran," *New Era*, Apr. 1976, 16.

11

HUMILITY: THE ULTIMATE DEFENSE

If pride is the overriding determinant that leads to apostasy, then it only makes sense that humility is the ultimate defense against becoming an apostate. Humility is such an important virtue—and so necessary to our spiritual growth—yet trying to determine whether or not you are acquiring humility can be incredibly difficult. While it may be hard to recognize humility in others, it is virtually impossible to measure it within ourselves. In fact, if you are not sure that you have humility, you probably do; and if you think, "Yes, I really am a humble person," there is a good chance that you might not be.

Concerning the elusive nature of humility, President Harold B. Lee wrote, "Someone has aptly said that humility is a rare virtue. When men become humble they soon become proud they're humble. I think there's a lot of that. Humility is one of the rarest qualities in all the world."[1] Elder Jack H. Goaslind said: "Humility is perhaps the most elusive quality we strive after. I say that because it seems to me that as soon as you begin to feel that you have humility, it's a pretty good indication that you may not."[2]

We have likely all known people who have tried to appear as though they were meek and mild, and perhaps they thought they were being humble. However, like President Lee pointed out, these people seem to be proud of their humility.

Perhaps one's very awareness of whether or not he is humble is a deterrent to becoming humble. We can ask God to help us develop humility, but I'm not certain that we can actually work at becoming humble. More likely, we work at becoming more obedient to God's commandments and more grateful for His many blessings. As we do these things we will be blessed with humility. And if we are doing these things with the right spirit, we won't really know that we are humble.

Elder Neal A. Maxwell wrote, "Meekness is not a display of humility; it is the real thing. True meekness is never proud of itself, never conscious of itself."[3] I also remember hearing what Elder Maxwell said about the humility of President Kimball. He said, "Meek President Spencer W. Kimball . . . did not realize how special he was."[4] That is true humility. President Kimball said, "When one becomes conscious of his great humility, he has already lost it. When one begins boasting of his humility, it has already become pride—the antithesis of humility."[5]

There is a great difference between those with the outward appearance of humility and those who are truly humble. Elder Richard G. Scott said, "We must cultivate true humility, not the ability to appear humble, but the sacred gift of true humility."[6] Humble people are very much aware of their weaknesses and their need for God's help. They will recognize their strengths too, but they will always acknowledge that these strengths are blessings from Heavenly Father and they give Him the credit for what they are able to accomplish.

What does it mean to have humility—to be a meek and humble servant of God? Elder Joseph B. Wirthlin said, "Humility is the recognition and attitude that one must rely on the Lord's assistance to make it through this life. We cannot endure to the end on our own strength. Without Him, we are nothing."[7] President Ezra Taft Benson wrote: "Humility! That does not mean weakness; that does not mean lack of courage, lack of faith, lack of self-confidence; but it means the recognition of a higher power upon which we are dependent."[8] At another time President Benson added, "In this work, we will never be successful unless we have that spirit of humility."[9]

Sometimes people confuse feelings of low self worth with humility, but nothing could be further from the truth. Elder Maxwell explained,

"Humility is not the disavowal of our worth; rather, it is the sober realization of how much we are valued by God. Nor does true humility call for the denigration of what truth we already know; rather, it is the catching of one's breath, as he realizes how very little that which we mortals presently know really is!"[10]

The experience that Moses had with Jehovah when Moses was caught up to an exceedingly high mountain, among other things, was a bestowal of the gift of humility upon the prophet. He had been raised in the grandeur of Egypt, a witness to the many great things that man could accomplish. But as he communicated with the Lord on the mount he saw the mighty works of God, His creations, and all the children of men, and Moses "greatly marveled and wondered."

When God's presence withdrew from Moses, in his weakened state he fell to the earth and did not receive his natural strength back "for the space of many hours." Moses then said to himself, "Now, for this cause I know that man is nothing, which thing I never had supposed" (Moses 1:10).

Moses did not learn that man is nothing to God but rather that man is nothing in comparison to God. The reality made known to Moses is that we are everything to God because we are His children. Moses became aware that he was a son of God and that with God's help, Moses had the potential to become like his Father in Heaven.

We are nothing in comparison to God. We can become like God. This is a comforting, yet humbling revelation. The strongest person, the smartest person, the most talented person, the most charitable person is no where near having the strength, intelligence, talent, and charity possessed by our Father in Heaven.

President Henry B. Eyring's father was a world-renowned scientist and a brilliant man. I read something he wrote that leads me to believe that he came to the same conclusion as Moses—that man truly is nothing in comparison to God no matter how smart the man is. Dr. Eyring wrote, "I suspect that if I asked you to name a scientist, you would think first of Albert Einstein. Certainly he was an extraordinarily able man." Dr. Eyring then mentioned that for thirteen of the years he was at

Princeton, Einstein was there too. He recalled, "In all that time I think I talked with him about ten hours." Dr. Eyring then shared one of his experiences with Albert Einstein:

> On one such occasion a man from the Navy and I spent the morning with Einstein at his home. . . . At noon we walked out into what had been a rose garden, but in wartime had been replanted as a victory garden. Now, I'm a farmer from Pima [Arizona], so I guessed what the crop was, but I didn't know whether Einstein knew or not. So I picked up a plant and asked him what it was. He didn't know. We walked about a hundred yards to where the gardener was sitting on his wheelbarrow. As I walked by, I asked him what it was. He said, "They're soybeans." Well, I thought what you would have thought: "Einstein doesn't know beans."[11]

Why is humility so important and what blessings are available to those who are truly humble? President Harold B. Lee said that "we have to be humble in order to have our prayers answered."[12] President James E. Faust wrote, "The only way to acquire spiritual knowledge and keep it burning brightly is to be humble, prayerful, and to strive diligently to keep all of the commandments."[13] Elder Marvin J. Ashton taught that "humility must be our foundation if the goodness of the Lord is to continue to come to and from us."[14] And President Spencer W. Kimball simply stated that "humility is the beginning of exaltation."[15]

Humility is also important when it comes to resisting temptation and repenting of our sins. President Henry B. Eyring wrote, "The very humility that is the sign of having been forgiven is protection against future sin. And it is by avoiding future sin that we retain a remission of the sins of the past."[16] One of the most serious sins that we should resist is the sin of pride. According to Elder Dallin H. Oaks, "Humility is the great protector. Humility is the antidote against pride. Humility is the catalyst for all learning, especially spiritual things."[17]

Earlier in this chapter I gave my opinion that trying to develop humility may not be the best way to actually receive the gift of being humble. As President Spencer W. Kimball noted, when a person becomes conscious of his humility, he has already lost it.[18] How do we become humble without being aware of our humility and risk losing it? President Kimball gives a wonderful response to that question:

> Somebody asked me [recently], "How do you keep humble? Sometimes I am humble and sometimes I am unhumble." How do you keep humble? I think there is a formula that will never fail. First, you evaluate yourself. What am I? I am the circle. I am the hole in the doughnut. I would be nothing without the Lord. My breath, my brains, my hearing, my sight, my locomotion, my everything depends upon the Lord. That is the first step and then we pray, and pray often, and we will not get up from our knees until we have communicated. The line may be down; we may have let it fall to pieces, but I will not get up from my knees until I have established communication—if it is twenty minutes, if it is all night like Enos. If it takes all day long, you stay on your knees until your unhumbleness has dissipated, until you feel the humble spirit and realize, "I could die this minute if it were not for the Lord's good grace. I am dependent upon him—totally dependent upon him," and then you read the scriptures.[19]

One of the most important keys to acquiring the gift of humility is the Spirit. Each of us has strengths and weaknesses. Strengths are blessings from God; gifts and talents we can use to bless the lives of others and build the kingdom of God. In our fallen state we also have inherent weakness. The Lord tells us that He gives "unto men weakness that they may be humble" (Ether 12:27).

Recognizing our strengths without seeing God's hand in our lives can lead to arrogance and pride. Recognizing those same strengths as gifts from God leads to humility because we must concede that without God's grace we can do nothing. When we have the Spirit we see "things as they really are" (Jacob 4:13).

When we closely examine our own shortcomings and failings without the Spirit it can be incredibly depressing. However, seeing those same weaknesses through the eyes of the Spirit can reveal to us how much we really need the help of our Father in Heaven. Instead of having feelings of loathing and low self-worth, we feel humbled and the Spirit gives us hope that with God's help we can overcome anything.

Strength + Spirit = Humility

Weakness + Spirit = Humility

How does humility help keep us safe from apostasy? Humility strengthens us to keep commandments. Being humble helps us remember the covenants we have made and the great blessings God has given us and will continue to bestow. Humility helps us see Church leaders in a positive light, protecting us from becoming fault-finders and complainers.

Seeing humility in others can open the door for the blessing of humility within us. Years ago I heard Hugh Nibley speak to a group of Church Educational System instructors and administrators. I had heard him speak a number of times before, but I had never seen him show any emotion. On this occasion he fought back the tears for a brief moment as he shared a personal experience about Spencer W. Kimball. Dr. Nibley said:

> I spent over a week with Apostle [Spencer W.] Kimball, visiting his home and stake in Arizona. We went by train in those far off days and on return we had a short stopover in Los Angeles. I visited some bookstores that I knew very well in the lower part of L.A., which were near the station. We only made it back to the train by running across the dusty vacant lot. I staggered into the drawing room with my arms full of a complete set of Molinos' work on probablism—the 16th century Jesuitical treatise in about twelve volumes. They were small. I greatly valued them. As we talked alone in the drawing room about the books, Brother Kimball casually took an immaculate linen handkerchief from the breast pocket in the his jacket and, stooping over, vigorously dusted off my shoes and trousers. It was the most natural thing in the world and we both took it completely for granted. After all, my shoes had gotten dusty in the race to the train and Brother Kimball had always told missionaries to keep themselves clean and proper. No great thing; . . . neither one of us said a thing about it. But ever since, that has been the thing that has conditioned my attitude toward the Brethren—what Brother Kimball did.[20]

In researching for this particular chapter, I read President Ezra Taft Benson's definitive discourse "Beware of Pride."[21] I remember thinking, "I wish President Benson had given a similar talk on humility." It occurred to me that since humility is the antithesis of pride, all I would have to do was use "Beware of Pride" as a template and write an inverted discourse focusing on humility. This was a great exercise for me in gaining a better understanding of humility.

Essentially, what I ended up with was a new talk by President Benson entitled "Seek for Humility." I sincerely hope that no one is offended by my efforts in rewriting "Beware of Pride."

SEEK FOR HUMILITY

I earnestly seek an interest in your faith and prayers as I strive to bring forth light on this Book of Mormon message—the virtue of humility. This message has been burning powerfully in my soul for some time. I know the Lord wants this message delivered now. In the premortal council, it was humility that kept those who followed God and Jesus Christ from falling and losing their first estate. At the end of the world, when God cleanses the earth by fire, the meek and humble will inherit the earth and the proud will be burned as stubble.

In the scriptures the Lord uses the following phrases: "he that shall humble himself shall be exalted" (Matthew 23:12); "be clothed with humility: for God . . . giveth grace to the humble" (1 Peter 5:5); "I would that ye should be humble, and be submissive and gentle" (Alma 7:23); "inasmuch as they were humble they might be made strong" (D&C 1:28). The Lord praises Moses as "meek above all men which were upon the face of the earth" (Numbers 12:3). Humility is a very misunderstood virtue, and many are humble without knowing it. There is no such thing as unrighteous humility—it is always considered a virtue. Therefore, no matter how the world uses the term, we must understand how God uses the term so we can understand the language of holy writ and profit thereby.

Most of us think of humility as modesty, unassuming nature, or meekness. All of these are elements of the virtue, but the heart, or core, is still missing. The central feature of humility is love—love toward God and love toward our fellowmen. Love means "charity, kindness to, or a state of caring." It is the power by which God wishes to guide us.

Humility is essentially submissive in nature. We accept the will of God over our own. When we direct our humility toward God, it is in the spirit of "not my will, but thine be done." As Paul said, "Charity suffereth long, and is kind; charity envieth not; charity vaunteth not itself, is not puffed up, doth not behave itself unseemly, seeketh not her own, is not easily provoked, thinketh no evil; rejoiceth not in iniquity, but rejoiceth in the truth" (1 Corinthians 13:4–6). Our will in submission to God's will allows desires, appetites, and passions to be controlled.

The humble can accept the authority of God giving direction to their lives. They get their perceptions of truth in the light of God's great knowledge, their abilities enhanced by God's priesthood power, their accomplishments as a result of God's gifts and blessings. Our love of God takes on many labels, such as being charitable, warm, kind, repentant, not easily offended, and faithful. The humble want to agree with God. They are eager to change their opinions to agree with God's knowledge. Another major portion of this less-than-prevalent virtue of humility is love toward our fellowmen. We should daily try to elevate others and help them feel good about themselves.

The humble make every man their friend by acknowledging and rejoicing in his works, gifts, talents, or any other God-given blessing. Paraphrasing C. S. Lewis: "Humility gets pleasure out of seeing that others can enjoy all blessings that are available; in raising a brother up to a better situation. Because there is no element of competition, there is humility." In the pre-earthly council, Jehovah accepted the proposed plan of the Father, became an advocate for it, and volunteered to become the sacrifice that was needed for the plan to be successful. He wished to have all honor and glory go to the Father. In short, his humble desire was to serve God.

The scriptures abound with evidences of the great blessings in consequence of the virtue of humility for individuals, groups, cities, and nations. Humility precedes growth and development. Humility would have saved the Nephite nation and the city of Sodom. It was through humility that the followers of Christ became His disciples. The humble Jews loved Jesus and accepted His claim to be the Son of God because He blessed their lives and would bring them salvation, and so they followed Him.

David became a friend to Saul through humility. He was not jealous because Saul was the king of Israel and had power and honor. The humble stand more in fear of God's judgment than of men's judgment. "What will God think of me?" weighs heavier than "What will men think of me?"

The king of the Lamanites was desirous to destroy Ammon, but when he saw the love that Ammon had for his son Lamoni, he asked to be taught the gospel. Lamoni had previously refused to harm Ammon because he felt Ammon's love and came to love him as well (see Alma 20:8–30).

Fear of God's judgment manifests itself in obedience to seek God's approval. The humble love "the praise of God more than the praise of men." Our motives for the things we do are where our humility is manifest. Jesus said He did "always those things" that pleased God (John 8:29). We would do well to have the pleasing of God as our motive rather than to try to elevate ourselves above our brother and outdo another.

Some humble people are not so concerned as to whether their wages meet their needs as they are that their wages are enough to help someone else. Their reward is helping others. This is the love of humility. When humility has a hold on our hearts, we gain our independence over the world and offer our agency to the righteousness of God's judgment. The whisperings of the Holy Ghost are more powerful than the shouting of the world. The revelations of God override the reasonings of men, and the humble will hold fast to the iron rod.

Humility is a virtue that can readily be seen in others but is rarely admitted in ourselves. Most of us consider humility to be a virtue of those in Church leadership positions, such as apostles and other general authorities, humbly leading us. There is, however, great humility among many of the average, every day Latter-day Saints, humbly serving the Lord in ways that are not always noticed. It is manifest in so many ways, such as service, magnifying callings, paying tithing and fast offerings, home and visiting teaching, and the sincere praise and building up of others.

Obedience is essentially being humbly submissive to someone in authority over us. It can be a parent, a priesthood leader, a teacher, or ultimately God. A humble person accepts the fact that someone is above him. He knows that this does not lower his position. Unselfishness is one of the more common faces of humility. "How everything affects others," is the center of all that matters—charity, empathy, sensitivity, spiritual fulfillment, and service.

Humility results in service organizations which are built up to bless others and benefit mankind. This fruit of the virtue of humility, namely charity, would have prevented the destruction of both the Jaredite and Nephite civilizations and could yet be the saving grace of many nations.

Another face of humility is harmony. Agreements, cooperation, support, marriages that last, family unity, compromise, and service all fall into this category of humility. Love in our families invites the Spirit of the Lord. It keeps our family members close to us. Harmony and unity range from a kind spoken word to worldwide peace. The scriptures tell us that "if ye are not one ye are not mine" (D&C 38:27).

The scriptures demonstrate that the humble are not easily offended and do not hold grudges. They freely forgive others for what might have caused injured feelings, inadvertent or otherwise. The humble receive counsel or correction easily. They are not defensive and they do not justify or rationalize their frailties and failures.

The humble depend on the Lord to tell them whether they have value or not. Their self-esteem is more of a spiritual awareness determined by their personal relationship with God. They feel worthwhile as individuals if they can reach out to others; and they are not threatened by the achievement, talent, beauty, or intellect of others. Humility is beautiful and powerful. It says, "If you succeed, I am sincerely happy for you." If we love God, do His will, and fear His judgment more than men's, we will have self-esteem.

Humility is an exalting virtue in the true sense of that word. It enhances or advances progression. The humble are easily taught. They will readily change their minds to accept truths, because to do so is to admit they have been incorrect and they desire to repent. Humility favorably affects all our relationships—our relationship with God and His servants, between husband and wife, parent and child, employer and employee, teacher and student, and all mankind. Our degree of humility determines how we treat our God and our brothers and sisters. Christ wants to lift us to where He is. Do we desire to do the same for others?

Humility strengthens our feelings of sonship to God and brotherhood to man. It does not separate and divide us by "ranks," according to our "riches" and our "chances for learning" (3 Nephi 6:12). Unity comes naturally for a humble people, and because we are one, we are the Lord's. Think of what humility has done for us in the past and how it is now blessing us in our lives, our families, and the Church.

Think of the repentance that could take place with lives changed, marriages preserved, and homes strengthened if humility motivated us to confess our sins and forsake them. Think of those who are totally active members of the Church because they refused to ever take offence and whose humility allows them to forgive and fully sup at the Lord's table.

Think of the tens of thousands of young men, women, and couples who are on missions because of humility that helped them yield their hearts unto God. Think of how much temple work is done because time spent in this godly service is important to people who have a humble desire to use their time to serve God.

Humility can affect all of us at various times and in various degrees. Now you can see why the humble people in Lehi's dream did not seek to enter the great and spacious building but remained faithfully at the tree.

Humility should be the universal virtue, the great attribute. Yes, humility should be the universal virtue, the great attribute. Humility—meekness, submissiveness—is the antidote for pride. It is the broken heart and contrite spirit. As Rudyard Kipling put it so well:

> The tumult and the shouting dies;
> The captains and the kings depart.
> Still stands thine ancient sacrifice,
> An humble and a contrite heart.
> Lord God of Hosts, be with us yet,
> Lest we forget, lest we forget.
> [*Hymns*, 1985, no. 80.]

God will have a humble people. Either we can choose to be humble or we can be compelled to be humble. Alma said, "Blessed are they who humble themselves without being compelled to be humble" (Alma 32:16).

Let us choose to be humble.

We can choose to humble ourselves by conquering enmity toward our brothers and sisters, esteeming them as ourselves, and lifting them as high or higher than we are (see D&C 38:24, 81:5, 84:106). We can choose to humble ourselves by receiving counsel and chastisement (see Jacob 4:10; Helaman 15:3; D&C 63:55, 101:4–5, 108:1, 124:61, 84, 136:31; Proverbs 9:8). We can choose to humble ourselves by forgiving those who have offended us (see 3 Nephi 13:11, 14; D&C 64:10). We can choose to humble ourselves by rendering selfless service (see Mosiah 2:16–17). We can choose to humble ourselves by going on missions and preaching the word that can humble others (see Alma 4:19, 31:5, 48:20). We can choose to humble ourselves by getting to the temple more frequently. We can choose to humble ourselves by confessing and forsaking our sins and being born of God (see D&C 58:43; Mosiah 27:25–26; Alma 5:7–14, 49). We can choose to humble ourselves by loving God, submitting our will to His and putting Him first in our lives (see 3 Nephi 11:11, 13:33; Moroni 10:32). Let us choose to be humble. We can do it. I know we can.

My dear brethren and sisters, we must prepare to redeem Zion. It was essentially the virtue of humility that would have allowed us to establish Zion in the days of the Prophet Joseph Smith. It was the same virtue that would have allowed consecration to continue among the Nephites.

Humility is the great stepping stone to Zion. I repeat: Humility is the great stepping stone to Zion. We must cleanse the inner vessel by embracing humility. We must yield "to the enticings of the Holy Spirit," put on the humble spiritual man, become "a saint through the atonement of Christ the Lord," and become "as a child, submissive, meek, humble" (Mosiah 3:19). That we may do so and go on to fulfill our divine destiny is my fervent prayer in the name of Jesus Christ, amen.

There has never been a greater act of humility than the Atonement of Jesus Christ. The Savior submitted His will completely to the Father. Elder Marlin K. Jensen said, "The greatest act of courage and love in the history of mankind—Christ's atoning sacrifice—was also the greatest act of humility and submissiveness."[22] It is not surprising that Jesus was completely submissive to his Father and demonstrated great humility in the presence of His Father. He said Himself, "My father is greater than I" (John 14:28).

Concerning the humility of Jesus Christ there is an interesting verse in the twelfth chapter of the Ether. The prophet Moroni writes: "And then shall ye know that I have seen Jesus, and that he hath talked with me face to face, and that he told me *in plain humility*, even as a man telleth another in mine own language concerning these things" (Ether 12:39, emphasis added).

Jesus Christ, the Son of God, the resurrected, exalted being with all power and all glory spoke to Moroni in plain humility. I have wondered if this has to do with Jesus speaking in Moroni's language rather than the language of heaven. Maybe He showed His humility by speaking to Moroni face to face. Is this an example of another of the Savior's perfected attributes?

Jesus obtained the fulness of the Father. All of His attributes are perfected. He has perfect love, perfect mercy, perfect understanding. I guess I just never really thought about Him having perfect humility, not just in the presence of His Father, but in the presence of His brothers and sisters, and those who are well beneath His level of glory.

That statement by Moroni astounds me. A statement by Hugh Nibley helped clarify this aspect of the Savior's perfected nature. Nibley wrote: "Humility is not a feeling of awe and reverence and personal unworthiness in the presence of overpowering majesty—anyone . . . confesses to being humble in the presence of God. Plain humility is reverence and respect in the presence of the lowest, not the highest, of God's creatures. Brigham Young said he often felt overawed in the presence of little children or any of his fellowmen—for in them he saw the image of his maker."[23]

Let us conclude this chapter on humility with a statement from President Gordon B. Hinckley:

> People ask me frequently what is my favorite verse of scripture. I have many and this is one of them, "Be thou humble; and the Lord thy God shall lead thee by the hand, and give thee answer to thy prayers" (D&C 112:10). What a promise to those who walk without arrogance, to those who walk without conceit, to those who walk without egotism, to those who walk humbly. "Be thou humble; and the Lord thy God shall lead thee by the hand, and give thee answers to thy prayers." What a solid and wonderful promise that is.[24]

NOTES

1. Lee, *Teachings of Harold B. Lee*, 617–18.
2. Jack H. Goaslind, "Be Honest, Be Pure, Be Humble," in *Speeches: Brigham Young University 1997–1998*, 133.
3. Neal A. Maxwell, "Meekly Drenched in Destiny," in *Speeches: Brigham Young University 1982–1983*, 4.
4. Neal A. Maxwell, "King Benjamin's Sermon: A Manual for Discipleship," F.A.R.M.S. Symposium, [BYU] April 13, 1996, 15; also see *That Ye May Believe*, 160.
5. Kimball, *Teachings of Spencer W. Kimball*, 233.
6. Richard G. Scott, "The Plan for Happiness and Exaltation," *Ensign*, Nov. 1981, 12.

7. Joseph B. Wirthlin, "Press On," *Ensign*, Nov. 2004, 104.
8. Benson, *So Shall Ye Reap*, 33–34.
9. Benson, *Teachings of Ezra Taft Benson*, 369–70.
10. Maxwell, *All These Things Shall Give Thee Experience*, 127.
11. Eyring, *Reflections of a Scientist*, 46–47.
12. Lee, *Teachings of Harold B. Lee*, 126.
13. James E. Faust, "It Can't Happen to Me," *Ensign*, May 2002, 48.
14. Marvin J. Ashton, "Neither Boast of Faith Nor of Mighty Works," *Ensign*, May 1990, 67.
15. Kimball, *Teachings of Spencer W. Kimball*, 215.
16. Eyring, *To Draw Closer to God*, 51.
17. Dallin H. Oaks, "Our Strengths Can Become Our Downfall," *Ensign*, Oct. 1994, 19.
18. Kimball, *Teachings of Spencer W. Kimball*, 233.
19. Ibid., 233–34.
20. Hugh Nibley, "Criticizing the Brethren," 1989 Church Educational System Doctrine and Covenants Symposium, 13–14. Another version of Nibley's experience is found in Nibley, *Brother Brigham Challenges the Saints*, 444.
21. Ezra Taft Benson, "Beware of Pride," *Ensign*, May 1989, 4–7.
22. Jensen, "To Walk Humbly With Thy God," *Ensign*, May 2001, 10.
23. Nibley, *Nibley on the Timely and Timeless*, 283–84.
24. Hinckley, *Teachings of Gordon B. Hinckley*, 265.

12

How to Deal with Apostates

Most of us have had encounters at one time or another with those who have abandoned their membership in the Church. Some have simply lost their faith and have left the Church with no bitterness toward the general membership, leaders, or doctrines. A number have become antagonistic toward certain Church members or leaders but feel no particular animosity toward the Church in general. A few have come to loathe anything related to The Church of Jesus Christ of Latter-day Saints—its doctrines, leaders, scriptures, or anyone who happens to be a member of the Church. They have become apostates.

The first thing we need to remember is that all people are children of God, they are our brothers and sisters, and that our Father in Heaven loves all of His children. Second, virtually everyone is capable of being redeemed. Elder Packer taught that except for a "few who defect to perdition, there is no habit, no addiction, no rebellion, no transgression, *no apostasy*, no crime exempted from the promise of complete forgiveness. That is the promise of the atonement of Christ."[1]

Unlike the parable of the wheat and the tares where wheat is wheat and tares are tares, in our Father in Heaven's plan of happiness tares can repent and become wheat. There are people who have abandoned the faith for a time but who have returned and become faithful again. We must never lose hope for our wayward brothers and sisters.

Third, we must never allow ourselves to be contentious. It can be incredibly frustrating to have our faith and beliefs attacked, especially by someone who is not only familiar with our doctrines, but who at one time actually believed in the things that we believe. Nevertheless, contention is of the devil and as soon as bitterness and anger appears the Spirit will depart.

It is difficult to maintain one's composure when the things we cherish and reverence are being trampled by a person who should know better. This is particularly true when the sacred nature of the House of the Lord is revealed and ridiculed. Again, patience, long-suffering, meekness, and love unfeigned are the keys to correctly handling attacks by apostates.

I have listened to and read personal attacks made against anti-Mormons by members of the Church. Despite some feelings of self-satisfaction and thinking *they're only getting what they deserve,* I recognize that these vindictive emotions are not of God. They emanate from the part of me that is the natural man—the part that is in opposition to what God wants me to become. I believe that anti-anti-Mormonism would in most cases qualify as contention.

In the Book of Mormon is recorded a situation where the Saints of that day were being persecuted by nonbelievers and apostates. There was a law in the Church that no person belonging to the Church should persecute those who did not belong to the Church. "Nevertheless, there were many among them who began to be proud, and began to contend warmly with their adversaries, even unto blows; yea, they would smite one another with their fists" (Alma 1:22).

It is interesting to see what happened to the Church members who contended with their adversaries. We read that "the hearts of many were hardened, and their names were blotted out, that they were remembered no more among the people of God. And also many withdrew themselves from among them" (Alma 1:24). Those Nephite Saints who became angry and bitter at being persecuted ended up out of the Church as apostates themselves.

Sampson Avard and the Danites

Sampson Avard was baptized by Orson Pratt in 1835 and arrived in Far West, Missouri, about June 1838. Avard was the creator of the

Danite Band, a group of Mormon men whose original purpose appears to have been to rid the Church from the influence of dissenters. The Danites then became a force designed to protect the Latter-day Saints from mob violence.

One former member of the Danites wrote that the group was created "for our personal defense; also of our families, property, and our religion."[2] Sampson Avard's personal motives for organizing the Danites are not entirely clear according to historian Leland Gentry. "At first he may have been prompted by a sincere desire to help protect the lives of the Saints . . . but he used the organization for other ends."[3]

It seems as though some of the Danites decided that the best defense was a good offense because they began to retaliate against those who committed violence against the Saints. The Danites would plunder, steal, and destroy property owned by those who they believed were doing the same things to the Mormons.

The Danite Band was very secretive in nature, and the men were required to swear solemn oaths to protect their secret order and to conceal the knowledge of their actions from the leaders of the Church. When Joseph Smith discovered what the Danites were doing he referred to their group as a secret combination that Avard had created "by which he might rise a mighty conqueror, at the expense and the overthrow of the Church."[4] Sampson Avard's case was brought before a Church court and he was excommunicated from the Church.

Despite the oaths of secrecy that Avard took and administered to others, when he was captured by General John B. Clark of the Missouri forces Avard quickly broke his "Danite Oath" and told *everything* to Clark. What he disclosed were falsehoods that incriminated Joseph Smith and other Church leaders and exonerated himself of all wrongdoing. The lies that he shared with the leaders of the Missouri militia were readily believed. Avard was never punished for any of his crimes.

Initially, Sampson Avard was concerned with eliminating dissenters and apostates from the Church. Ultimately, his anger, belligerence, and dishonesty resulted in Avard becoming an apostate. Although the Danites existed for only a short time in northern Missouri, some anti-Mormons today accuse the Church of having modern-day Danites that do the secret bidding of Church leaders. It is amazing how the Church continues to suffer repercussions from the actions of Sampson Avard.

Brigham Young and Sidney Rigdon

A positive example of dealing with an apostate comes from the life of Brigham Young. After the death of the Prophet Joseph Smith, Sidney Rigdon offered to serve as guardian of the Church at the same time as Brigham Young asserted that the Twelve had the keys of the priesthood and should lead the Church. At a conference where both Rigdon and Young spoke, those Church members present were unanimous in sustaining Brigham Young and the Twelve.

Rigdon and a few others who supported him also sustained the Twelve in public at the conference that day, but privately they took action to undermine the leadership of the Twelve and promote their own interests. Brigham Young heard rumors about what Sidney Rigdon was doing and he, along with Orson Hyde, went to Rigdon's home to visit with him. "We went into his house," said Brigham Young, "and after the usual compliments, I sat down directly opposite him, and took hold of his hand." He then asked Brother Rigdon some very direct questions about his actions and discovered that Sidney Rigdon believed that he had keys and authority above any other man, including the Twelve. Brother Brigham also confirmed that the previous evening Rigdon had ordained a number of men as prophets, priests, and kings.[5]

Sidney Rigdon was summoned to appear before a Church court, and although he refused to attend, the hearing was held and Rigdon was excommunicated from the Church. This action was an ecclesiastical responsibility, not a personal vendetta. Brigham Young said of Rigdon:

> I am willing that you should know that my feelings for Sidney Rigdon as a man, as a private citizen, are of the best kind. I have loved that man and always had the very best feelings for him; I have stood in defense of his life and his house in Kirtland, and have lain on the floor, night after night, and week after week, to defend him. There are those who are following Sidney for whom my heart is grieved, I

esteem them as good citizens. But when it touches the salvation of the people, I am the man that walks to the line.[6]

Do Not Allow Yourself to Be Influenced by Apostates

This brings us to another important aspect of dealing with apostates. Amidst the love, kindness, patience, and hope that we must have for them, we must never allow ourselves to be influenced by them to the detriment of our own faith and testimony. Each situation is different and so we must prayerfully approach our options and be guided by the Spirit.

It sounds harsh to consider ignoring an individual or even severing ties with someone we love. Hopefully, it will never come to that, but there may be circumstances where continuing an association will drag us down. An analogy can be made to the Savior's counsel: "Wherefore if thy hand or thy foot offend thee, cut them off, and cast them from thee: it is better for thee to enter into life halt or maimed, rather than having two hands or two feet to be cast into everlasting fire. And if thine eye offend thee, pluck it out, and cast it from thee: it is better for thee to enter into life with one eye, rather than having two eyes to be cast into hell fire" (Matthew 18:8–9).

The Joseph Smith Translation of the verses mentioned above adds the following: "And a man's hand is his friend, and his foot also; and a man's eye, are they of his own household" (JST Matthew 18:9).

At times we might be approached by some apostate Mormons who are handing out literature that is denigrating our Church, its doctrine, and its leaders. Typically, the best thing to do is to pay no attention to the material or the person. Elder Bruce R. McConkie wrote:

> Ignore, if you can, the endless array of anti-Mormon literature and avoid cults like a plague. Conversion is not born of contention. He that hath the spirit of contention is not of God (Prov. 18:6; Rom. 2:7–8; 1 Cor. 11:16; James 3:16; 3 Ne. 11:29; D&C 10:63). Our divine commission is to declare glad tidings to the world, not to quarrel with others about the meaning of texts. There are, of course, answers to all of the false claims of those who array themselves against us—I do not believe the devil has had a new idea for a hundred years—but

> conversion is not found in the dens of debate. It comes rather to those who read the Book of Mormon in the way Moroni counseled. Most members of the Church would be better off if they simply ignored the specious claims of the professional anti-Mormons.[7]

Elder Marvin J. Ashton shared an experience he had in dealing with a situation where anti-Mormon literature was flooding a particular area of a mission. He said that he heard about the circumstances shortly before he was to visit the missionaries in that area. He recalled that when he arrived the missionaries were anxious to show him some of the material that was being distributed. "They were disturbed by the accusations," he said, "and were eager to plan retaliation."[8]

> The elders sat on the edge of their chairs as I read the slander and false declarations issued by a minister who apparently felt threatened by their presence and successes. As I read the pamphlet containing the malicious and ridiculous statements, I actually smiled, much to the surprise of my young associates. When I finished, they asked, "What do we do now? How can we best counteract such lies?"
>
> I answered, "To the author of these words, we do nothing. We have no time for contention. We only have time to be about our Father's business. Contend with no man. Conduct yourselves as gentlemen with calmness and conviction and I promise you success."[9]

Some of the most bitter enemies of the Church are those who were once part of the fellowship of the Saints. Elder Neal A. Maxwell wrote, "No attacks on the Church will be more bitter or more persistent . . . no taunts will be more shrill than those of apostates and excommunicants."[10]

Harsh criticism from former members can be especially damaging to those who know very little about The Church of Jesus Christ of Latter-day Saints. After all, are not these people "insiders"—people who should know? Someone once gave me an anti-Mormon book that on the cover declared that the author was "A Former Deacon of the Mormon Church." While that title might carry some weight in other faiths, there are not many deacons that I would consider to be "in the know" as far as Church matters are concerned.

Even those who have worked for the Church or served in some of the weightier callings such as bishop, Relief Society president, or stake president cannot be considered "insiders" any more than the rank and file of the Church. Position in Church leadership or the privilege of working full-time for the kingdom does not give anyone an advantage in receiving exaltation. An article in the *Millennial Star* stated: "We cannot think that our ordinations or appointments have necessarily advanced us one particle towards celestial life, only so far as we have made them do it, by taking advantage of the rich opportunities they have put within our hands to learn and get an insight into the real sources of celestial life. Ordinations do not celestialize; appointments do not elevate: they only authorize us to be channels of light to others and to ourselves, if we will."[11]

I have known of ward and stake leaders and educators formerly employed by the Church who have apostatized. Position in the Church does not provide a better view of Church doctrines and principles than is available to the average member, and leadership callings do not save. I have taught for the Church Educational System for over thirty years and, trust me, that does not make me an insider by any stretch of the imagination.

Forgiveness and Hope

We need to show love and patience for those who have wandered from the path, even if they are antagonistic and combative. While we cannot force them to see their error, we can "leave a light on for them" and help them feel that they are always welcome to come home. We must never lose hope for God's wayward children.

Harvey Whitlock was one of the first high priests of this dispensation. He served the Lord faithfully as a missionary, but by about 1834 Whitlock had apostatized from the Church.[12] In September 1835 he wrote a letter to Joseph Smith asking the Prophet to inquire of the Lord on his behalf. Whitlock wanted to return to the Church and wrote that he would "covenant to abide the word that may be given, for I am willing to receive any chastisement that the Lord sees I deserve."[13]

Joseph responded the very day he received Whitlock's letter. In his letter of reply Joseph noted that he had read the letter that he had received from Whitlock twice and it had given him sensations "better imagined than described." Joseph wrote, "The very flood gates of my heart were broken up—I could not refrain from weeping. I thank God that it has entered into your heart to try to return to the Lord."[14]

The Prophet then went on to say that he had indeed inquired of the Lord concerning Whitlock and had received a revelation. In part, the revelation stated:

> Verily, thus saith the Lord unto you—Let him who was my servant Harvey, return unto me, and unto the bosom of my Church, and forsake all the sins wherewith he has offended against me, and pursue from henceforth a virtuous and upright life, and remain under the direction of those whom I have appointed to be pillars and heads of my Church. And behold, saith the Lord your God, his sins shall be blotted out from under heaven, and shall be forgotten from among men, and shall not come up in mine ears, nor be recorded as a memorial against him, but I will lift him up, as out of deep mire, and he shall be exalted upon the high places.[15]

Joseph concluded his letter to Harvey Whitlock by pointing out the willingness of our Heavenly Father to "forgive sins, and restore to favor all those who are willing to humble themselves before Him, and confess their sins, and forsake them, and return to Him." He told Whitlock that "the angels rejoice over you, while the Saints are willing to receive you again into fellowship."[16] Harvey Whitlock returned to Kirtland and was rebaptized January 30, 1836.

An even greater example of the Prophet Joseph's willingness to forgive apostates is the case of W. W. Phelps. Joining the Church in June 1831, William Wines Phelps became a prominent figure in early Church history. He is probably best remembered for being the editor of the first Church-owned newspaper *The Evening and the Morning Star* and for writing a number of hymns, including "Now Let Us Rejoice," and "The Spirit of God Like a Fire is Burning."

Although Phelps had been a trusted associate of Joseph Smith, in 1838 he went through some difficult trials, became bitter toward Joseph and the Church, and "joined the apostates and oppressors who sought the Prophet's life."[17]

That year Phelps testified against Church leaders at a military court held in Richmond, Missouri. For his betrayal and apostasy Phelps was excommunicated in March 1839.

In June 1840 W. W. Phelps wrote to Joseph Smith and asked if he might be forgiven and reunite with the Church. The Prophet's reply is dated July 22, 1840, and is beautiful in its warm-hearted quality. The following are excerpts from that letter:

> It is true, that we have suffered much in consequence of your behavior—the cup of gall, already full enough for mortals to drink, was indeed filled to overflowing when you turned against us. One with whom we had oft taken sweet counsel together, and enjoyed many refreshing seasons from the Lord—"had it been an enemy, we could have borne it." . . . However, the cup has been drunk, the will of our Father has been done, and we are yet alive, for which we thank the Lord. And having been delivered from the hands of wicked men by the mercy of our God, we say it is your privilege to be delivered from the powers of the adversary, be brought into the liberty of God's dear children, and again take your stand among the Saints. . . . Believing your confession to be real, and your repentance genuine, I shall be happy once again to give you the right hand of fellowship, and rejoice over the returning prodigal.[18]

Joseph then concluded his letter with this short rhyme:

> "Come on, dear brother, since the war is past,
> For friends at first, are friends again at last."[19]

NOTES

1. Boyd K. Packer, "The Brilliant Morning of Forgiveness," *Ensign*, Nov. 1995, 20 (emphasis added).
2. Luman Andros Shurtliff "Diary," 120, as cited in Leland H. Gentry, "The Danite Band of 1838," *BYU Studies*, vol. 14, no. 4 (Summer 1974), 428.
3. Leland H. Gentry, "The Danite Band of 1838," *BYU Studies*, vol. 14, no. 4 (Summer 1974), 437.
4. Smith, *History of the Church*, 3:179.

5. "Trial of Elder Rigdon," *Times and Seasons*, Sept. 15, 1844, vol. 5, 648.
6. Ibid.
7. McConkie, *Doctrines of the Restoration: Sermons and Writings of Bruce R. McConkie*, 233.
8. Marvin J. Ashton, "No Time for Contention," *Ensign*, May 1978, 7.
9. Ibid.
10. Maxwell, *Wherefore, Ye Must Press Forward*, 79.
11. E. L. T. Harrison, "A Real Representative of the Most High," *Millennial Star*, vol. 41, October 9, 1858, 643. This is an excellent article about the importance of understanding that it is the Atonement of Jesus Christ and our willingness to follow the will of God that saves—not position or calling. Harrison later lost sight of the fact that we follow the will of God as we follow His chosen prophet. Sadly, Harrison became disgruntled with Brigham Young's leadership and became an apostate.
12. *Teachings of the Presidents of the Church: Joseph Smith*, 75.
13. Smith, *History of the Church*, 2:314.
14. Ibid., 314–15.
15. Ibid., 315.
16. Ibid.
17. Boyd K. Packer, "The Mantle is Far, Far Greater Than the Intellect," *BYU Studies*, vol. 21, no. 3 (Summer 1981), 276.
18. Smith, *History of the Church*, 4:163.
19. Ibid., 164.

Conclusion

Our Father in Heaven has made sure that agency always exists. For us to grow and progress there must be freedom of choice, and there must be choices. In addition to the choices that God inspires us to select—choices that lead to liberty and eternal life—there are also choices that lead to captivity and death—enticements by Satan. This is the necessary opposition in all things spoken of by father Lehi (2 Nephi 2:11).

Apostasy is the incorrect use of agency through rejecting God's truth after having initially accepted it. There have always been those who have forsaken the true plan of our Father in Heaven. This was true in our premortal existence and during every dispensation since the fall of Adam. Apostasy has and will exist during our own dispensation of the fulness of times.

Joseph Smith taught that before we joined the Church we stood on neutral ground, and when the gospel was presented to us and good and evil were set before us, we were free to choose. However, when we joined the Church we enlisted to serve God and "when you did that you left neutral ground, and you never can get back on to it." Joseph said that "should you forsake the Master you enlisted to serve, it will be by the instigation of the evil one, and you will follow his dictation and be his servant."[1]

Those who have made covenants to serve God, but have then chosen to break those covenants and fight against God's kingdom here on the earth have become apostates and enemies to God's kingdom and His servants. Apostates are not always clearly recognized, for they do not all leave the Church or blatantly fight against it. There are those who have secretly apostatized and remained within the Church believing they can do more damage from the inside. Ezra Taft Benson warned that "not only are there apostates within our midst, but there are also apostate doctrines taught in our classes and from our pulpits . . . and these apostate precepts of men cause our people to stumble."[2]

The gospel of Jesus Christ was restored to the earth through the Prophet Joseph Smith and has remained intact through the keys of the priesthood held by each succeeding prophet. The majority of those religious organizations that broke away as alternatives to the restored Church have disappeared. Brigham Young boldly stated, "All that want to draw a party from the church after them, let them do it if they can, but they will not prosper. If any man thinks he has influence among this people to lead away a party, let him try it, and he will find out that there is power with the apostles which will carry them victorious through all the world."[3]

Schisms from our Church or groups basing their doctrines on portions of the truth restored through Joseph Smith still appear periodically, but most cease to exist within a short time. The churches that remain will not continue to grow or prosper for any extended length of time.

Then there are the apostates who bitterly leave the Church, not because they think they have found something better, but simply to renounce and attack what they once believed. They harshly criticize the teachings, doctrines, and leaders of The Church of Jesus Christ of Latter-day Saints. Korihor-like, they accuse Church leaders "of leading away the people after the silly traditions of their fathers, for the sake of glutting on the labors of the people" (Alma 30:31).

In the minds of these apostates the Church is not just another religion, but some type of evil organization secretly trying to undermine society and attempting to drag souls down to hell. This type of apostate is frequently very vocal and seeks publicity, and their rants often appear in newspapers, books, and in broadcast media. I used to be greatly troubled when enemies of the Church made news on the national stage. However, I have discovered that no matter how ugly or widespread the attack, within a short time both the controversy and the person seem to fade away.

President Gordon B. Hinckley spoke of those "who with the sophistry of beguiling words and clever design will spread doubt and seek to undermine the foundation on which this cause is established." He said that they may have their day in the sun; their brief season of "plaudits of the doubters and the skeptics and the critics, but they will fade and be forgotten as have their kind in the past." President Hinckley concluded, "Meanwhile, we shall go forward, regardless of their criticism, aware of but undeterred by their statements and actions."[4]

We have no concern for the continuing existence and expansion of the Lord's Church. It has been restored in the latter days and will continue to grow until it fills the whole earth. God's kingdom will not be lost from the earth again. Elder McConkie likened the Church to a great caravan. There will be yapping dogs snapping at the heels of weary travelers and there will be predators that will "claim those few who fall by the way," but the caravan will move on.[5]

It is not the well-being of the Church that is the concern. Rather, it is the predators and those who might fall by the way that is troubling. We do not want to lose any member of the Church to apostasy. Tragically, we know that some will inevitably be lost. We also know that a few of those that are lost actually become predators, seeking to destroy the faith of others. President Hinckley said that "there are still those, not a few, who criticize and rebel, who apostatize and lift their voices against this work. We have always had them. . . . I suppose we always will have them as long as we are trying to do the work of the Lord."[6]

We need to be awake to the fact that apostasy does exist in our time within our Church. Elder Bruce R. McConkie wrote, "It is assumed, in an unthinking sort of way, that Israel was scattered in ancient days and is being gathered in modern times. In reality, the scattering of Israel is still going on."[7] Part of this scattering is a result of personal apostasy. It might be surprising to average Latter-day Saints how many times they will have contact with apostates from the Church. Even more surprising might be to discover who among our current Church membership are disgruntled and bitter. They have lost their faith in the restored gospel but for one reason or another have maintained their membership.

I have heard more than a few apostate comments made in Church meetings. These were not false doctrines accidentally shared by people who were mistaken in their understanding. These remarks were made by people with an agenda contrary to revealed truths.

I remember attending a sacrament meeting where a man who had just moved into the ward spoke about the history of polygamy. It was not blatantly obvious that he did not believe Wilford Woodruff was acting under the direction of God when plural marriage was discontinued. But he left room for other possibilities and attempted to instill doubt in the minds of the congregation. At the conclusion of the man's remarks, the bishop thanked the speakers and then reminded his ward that anyone practicing plural marriage in our day would be excommunicated. It was not surprising when a few years later the man who had spoken was excommunicated for practicing plural marriage.

We must protect ourselves and our families from the apostasy of the latter days. Each person must acquire his or her own testimony through the means the Lord has designed: prayer, obedience, scripture study, service, and following the will of God. We must be consistent in our efforts to keep our testimonies alive and growing. President Harold B. Lee remarked, "Testimony is as elusive as a moonbeam; it's as fragile as an orchid; you have to recapture it every morning of your life. You have to hold on by study, and by faith, and by prayer."[8]

Conviction to the gospel of Jesus Christ is a protection from the apostasy happening in our day. The Church of Jesus Christ of Latter-day Saints is not just another religion. It is God's kingdom on the earth and "the only true and living church upon the face of the whole earth" (D&C 1:30). We cannot pick and choose only selected parts of restored truth to believe. We must be converted to the entire gospel.

Occasionally, the idea is promoted by a Church member that even if

Joseph Smith lied about the First Vision or wrote the Book of Mormon and made up the story about golden plates, the Church is still a good organization because of its focus on family, welfare, and service to others. I have actually heard the Book of Mormon referred to as "inspired fiction." These are apostate thoughts. Elder Jeffrey R. Holland pulled no punches in his view of this kind of thinking. To a group of religious educators he said: "Let's not have any of the embarrassingly silly pap we have heard from some recently about Joseph earnestly 'thinking' he saw an angel and 'imagining' he translated from a set of gold plates. Excuse me if I am speechless—absolutely, totally, and bewilderingly incredulous—at such a comment. Is that really said with a straight face? . . . That whole suggestion simply adds insult to infamy."[9]

Elder Holland compared these types of theories among Latter-day Saints with the way C. S. Lewis saw people from various Christian religions who questioned the divinity of Jesus Christ. Lewis wrote:

> I am trying here to prevent anyone saying the really foolish thing that people often say about Him: [that is] "I'm ready to accept Jesus as a great moral teacher, but I don't accept his claim to be God." That is the one thing we must not say. A man who was merely a man and said the sort of things Jesus said would not be a great moral teacher. He would either be a lunatic—on a level with the man who says he is a poached egg—or else he would be the Devil of Hell. You must make your choice. Either this man was, and is, the son of God: or else a madman or something worse. You can shut Him up for a fool, you can spit at Him and kill Him as a demon; or you can fall at His feet and call Him Lord and God. But let us not come with any patronizing nonsense about His being a great human teacher. He has not left that open to us. He did not intend to.[10]

President J. Reuben Clark taught that "there are for the Church and for each and all of its members, two prime things which may not be overlooked, shaded, or discarded." These two fundamental beliefs are first: Jesus Christ is the Son of God and Savior of the world. Second, that Joseph Smith was literally visited by the Father and the Son and that through the Prophet Joseph the holy order of priesthood and the gospel was restored. Also, that Joseph Smith translated the Book of Mormon by the gift and power of God and "that the Book of Mormon is just what it professes to be."[11] In the April 2003 general conference President Gordon B. Hinckley stated, "Each of us has to face the matter—either the Church is true, or it is a fraud. There is no middle ground. It is the Church and kingdom of God, or it is nothing."[12]

We must protect our families from latter day apostasy by teaching them the gospel in the home. There needs to be family scripture study, family home evening, and family gospel discussions. We shield our families from false doctrine when they have been taught true doctrine. Teaching our families the gospel also includes watching general conference together, attending church as families, serving faithfully in callings we receive, paying our tithes and offerings, and doing all else that our Father in Heaven requires of us.

We may not think that little things like missing family prayer or staying home from church to watch the Super Bowl can damage our spirituality or negatively affect our families, but small things add up. President Hinckley reminded us that it is "often the very small and singularly inconsequential acts of our lives that eventually make so great a difference. . . . The history of this church is replete with cases of men who started on the road to apostasy with small, seemingly unimportant decisions."[13]

We must remember the success experiences we have observed in Church history where apostates have returned to the fold. Our Father in Heaven continues to reach out for his rebellious children. The Savior reminded the children of Israel how often He had tried to gather them "as a hen gathereth her chickens under her wings," but they had refused to return to Him. He then said, "how often *will I gather you* as a hen gathereth her chickens under her wings, if ye will repent and return unto me with full purpose of heart" (3 Nephi 10:4–6). "There is never a time," taught the Prophet Joseph, "when the spirit is too old to approach God. All are within the reach of pardoning mercy, who have not committed the unpardonable sin."[14]

Many of us have loved ones who have strayed from the path of righteousness. In most cases, this would not be considered full-fledged apostasy. Rather, most have merely strayed in ignorance for a time. "God is merciful to ignorance," taught Elder Orson F. Whitney. "Only the fulness of knowledge brings the fulness of accountability. Our Heavenly Father is far more merciful, infinitely more charitable, than even the best of his servants, and the Everlasting Gospel is mightier in power to save than our narrow finite minds can comprehend."[15]

We must not lose hope for those who have wandered away from the faith. Luke chapter fifteen contains three examples given by the Savior of things that are lost being found—the lost sheep, the missing coin, and the prodigal son. They all end up back where they are supposed to be. Whether a person wanders away, is lost through neglect, or purposely rebels, they can come back. They may return during mortality or in the life to come, but we must not lose hope, for the Lord has provided a way for their return.[16]

Finally, we need to be aware that any of us can lose our way or rebel and become enemies to the Lord's work if we do not watch ourselves and make the efforts to become and remain strong. We cannot allow ourselves to be influenced by those who have become enemies to the Church and who seek to drag others down with them.

We must faithfully endure to the end. Shortly after Elder M. Russell Ballard returned from the mission field he had a conversation with a ninety-year-old stake patriarch who told Elder Ballard, "I pray every night that God will see me safely dead with my testimony burning brightly." When the young Elder Ballard said that he doubted that anyone was better prepared than the patriarch to whom he was speaking, the faithful old man replied, "My boy, no one is safe until he has endured to the very end of his life."[17]

We live in a difficult day and age. Yet we are greatly blessed to have the restored gospel of Jesus Christ and to enjoy the peace and happiness and safety that God's restored kingdom offers us. The adversary does all that he can to drag us away from the correct path. May we be vigilant in keeping our covenants, the commandments, and following the will of our Father until we are safely dead with our testimonies burning brightly.

NOTES

1. "Recollections of the Prophet Joseph Smith," *Juvenile Instructor,* vol. 28, number 16, Aug. 15, 1892, 492.
2. Ezra Taft Benson, "To the Humble Followers of Christ," *Improvement Era,* June 1969, 43.
3. Roberts, *Comprehensive History of the Church,* 2:417.
4. Hinckley, *Teachings of Gordon B. Hinckley,* 124–25.
5. Bruce R. McConkie, "The Caravan Moves On," *Ensign,* Nov. 1984, 85.
6. Gordon B. Hinckley, "Remember . . . Thy Church, O Lord," *Ensign,* May 1996, 83.
7. McConkie, *A New Witness for the Articles of Faith,* 520.
8. Lee, *Teachings of Harold B. Lee,* 139.
9. Jeffrey R. Holland, "A Standard Unto My People," CES Symposium on the Book of Mormon, 9 August 1994, 3–4.
10. Lewis, *Mere Christianity,* 55–56. Quoted by Holland, "A Standard Unto My People," 4.
11. J. Reuben Clark, "The Charted Course of the Church in Education," published in Packer, *Teach Ye Diligently,* Revised Edition, 362–63.
12. Gordon B. Hinckley, "Loyalty," *Ensign,* May 2003, 60.
13. Gordon B. Hinckley, "Don't Drop the Ball," *Ensign,* Nov. 1994, 48–49.
14. Smith, *Teachings of the Prophet Joseph Smith,* 191.
15. Orson F. Whitney, in Conference Report, Apr. 1929, 110.
16. Ibid.
17. "Priesthood Holders United Throughout World in Fellowship of Service," *LDS Church News,* May 9, 1992, 8.

BIBLIOGRAPHY

Backman, Milton V., Jr. *The Heavens Resound: A History of the Latter-day Saints in Ohio 1830–1838*. Salt Lake City: Deseret Book, 1983.

Ballard, M. Russell. *When Thou Art Converted—Continuing Our Search for Happiness*. Salt Lake City: Deseret Book, 1983.

Barrett, Ivan J. *Joseph Smith and the Restoration*. Revised ed. Provo, Utah: Brigham Young University Press, 1973.

Benson, Ezra Taft. *So Shall Ye Reap*. Salt Lake City: Deseret Book, 1960.

———. *Teachings of Ezra Taft Benson*. Salt Lake City: Bookcraft, 1988.

Bringhurst, Newell G. and John C. Hamer, eds. *Scattering of the Saints: Schism within Mormonism*. Independence, Missouri: John Whitmer Books, 2007.

Britsch, R. Lanier. *Unto the Islands of the Sea*. Salt Lake City: Deseret Book, 1986.

Cannon, George Q. *Gospel Truth: Discourses and Writings of George Q. Cannon*. 2 vols. Selected, arranged, and edited by Jerald L. Newquist. Salt Lake City: Deseret Book, 1974.

Carter, Kate B. *Our Pioneer Heritage*, vol. 5. Salt Lake City: Daughters of the Utah Pioneers, 1962.

Church Educational System. *The Charge to Religious Educators*, 1st edition. Salt Lake City: The Church of Jesus Christ of Latter-day Saints, 1981.

Clark, James R., compiler. *Messages of the First Presidency*, 6 vols. Salt Lake City: Bookcraft, 1965–75.

Conference Reports of the Church of Jesus Christ of Latter-day Saints. Salt Lake

City: The Church of Jesus Christ of Latter-day Saints, 1898 to present.

Edwards, Paul M. *Our Legacy of Faith: A Brief History of the Reorganized Church of Jesus Christ of Latter Day Saints*. Independence, Missouri: Herald Publishing House, 1991.

Eyring, Henry. *Reflections of a Scientist*. Salt Lake City: Deseret Book, 1983.

Eyring, Henry B. *To Draw Closer to God*. Salt Lake City: Deseret Book, 1997.

Ferrell, James L. *The Peacegiver*. Salt Lake City: Deseret Book, 2004.

Fife, Austin and Alta. *Saints of Sage and Saddle: Folklore Among the Mormons*. Bloomington, Indiana: Indiana University Press, 1956.

Fitzpatrick Doyle, *The King Strang Story*. Lansing, Michigan: National Heritage, 1970.

Fletcher, Rupert J. and Daisy Whiting. *Alpheus Cutler and the Church of Jesus Christ*. Independence, Missouri: The Church of Jesus Christ, 1974.

Flint, B. C. *An Outline History of the Church of Christ (Temple Lot)*. 3rd ed. revised. Independence, Missouri: The Board of Publications The Church of Christ (Temple Lot), 1979.

Garr, Arnold K. and Clark V. Johnson, eds. *Regional Studies in Latter-day Saint Church History*. Provo, Utah: Brigham Young University, Department of Church History and Doctrine, 1994.

Gaskill, Alonzo L. *The Savior and the Serpent*. Salt Lake City: Deseret Book, 2005.

Hinckley, Gordon B. *Teachings of Gordon B. Hinckley*. Salt Lake City: Deseret Book, 1997.

Jackson, Kent P., ed. *Studies in Scripture: 1 Kings to Malachi*. Salt Lake City: Deseret Book, 1993.

Journal of Discourses. 26 volumes. London: Latter-day Saints' Book Depot, 1854–86.

Kimball, Spencer W. *Miracle of Forgiveness*. Salt Lake City: Bookcraft, 1969.

———. *Teachings of Spencer W. Kimball*. Edited by Edward L. Kimball. Salt Lake City: Bookcraft, 1982.

Launius, Roger D. *Joseph Smith III: Pragmatic Prophet*. Chicago: University of Illinois Press, 1988.

Launius, Roger D. and W. B. Spillman, eds. *Let Contention Cease*. Independence, Missouri: Graceland/Park Press, 1991.

Lee, Harold B. *The Teachings of Harold B. Lee*. Clyde J. Williams, ed. Salt Lake City: Bookcraft, 1996.

Leonard, Glen M. *Nauvoo: A Place of Peace, A People of Promise*. Salt Lake City: Deseret Book Company and Provo, Utah: Brigham Young University Press, 2002.

Lewis, C. S. *Mere Christianity*. New York: Colliers Books, 1960.

Ludlow, Daniel H., ed. *Encyclopedia of Mormonism*, 4 vols. New York: Macmillan Publishing Company, 1992.

———. *Latter-day Prophets Speak*. Salt Lake City: Bookcraft, 1988.

Maxwell, Neal A. *All These Things Shall Give Thee Experience*. Salt Lake City: Deseret Book, 1979.

———. *Deposition of a Disciple*. Salt Lake City: Deseret Book, 1976.

———. *Meek and Lowly*. Salt Lake City: Deseret Book, 1987.

———. *That Ye May Believe*. Salt Lake City: Bookcraft, 1992.

———. *Wherefore Ye Must Press Forward*. Salt Lake City: Deseret Book, 1977.

McConkie, Bruce R. *A New Witness for the Articles of Faith*. Salt Lake City: Deseret Book, 1985.

———. *Doctrines of the Restoration: Sermons and Writings of Bruce R. McConkie*. Edited by Mark L. McConkie. Salt Lake City: Bookcraft, 1989.

———. *Mormon Doctrine*, second edition. Salt Lake City: Bookcraft, 1966.

McConkie, Mark L., comp. and ed. *Remembering Joseph*. Salt Lake City: Deseret Book, 2003. The book also came with a CD-ROM with material not contained in the printed text.

McKay, David O. *Pathways to Happiness*. Llewelyn R. McKay, comp. Salt Lake City: Bookcraft, 1957.

Nibley, Hugh. *Brother Brigham Challenges the Saints*. Edited by Don E. Norton and Shirley S. Ricks. Salt Lake City: Deseret Book and Provo, Utah: Foundation for Ancient Research and Mormon Studies, 1994.

———. *Nibley on the Timely and Timeless*. Provo, Utah: Religious Studies Center, Brigham Young University, 1978.

———. *The Old Testament and Related Studies*. Salt Lake City: Deseret Book and Provo, Utah: Foundation for Ancient Research and Mormon Studies, 1986.

Oaks, Dallin H. *The Lord's Way*. Salt Lake City: Deseret Book, 1991.

Packer, Boyd K. *Let Not Your Heart Be Troubled.* Salt Lake City: Bookcraft, 1991.

———. *Teach Ye Diligently.* Salt Lake City: Deseret Book, 1975.

Pratt, Orson. *The Orson Pratt Journals.* Compiled and Arranged by Elden J. Watson. Salt Lake City: Elden J. Watson, 1975.

Quinn, D. Michael. "The Mormon Succession Crisis of 1844." *BYU Studies* 16 (Winter 1976): 187–233. Provo, Utah: Brigham Young University Press, 1976.

Rich, Russell R. *Little Known Schisms of the Restoration.* 3rd ed. Provo, Utah: Brigham Young University, 1967.

———. *Those Who Would Be Leaders: Offshoots of Mormonism,* second edition. Provo, Utah: Brigham Young University Press, 1967.

Roberts, B. H. *A Comprehensive History of The Church of Jesus Christ of Latter-day Saints.* 6 volumes. Provo, UT: Brigham Young University Press, 1965.

Shields, Steven L. *Divergent Paths of the Restoration.* 3rd ed. revised and enlarged. Bountiful, Utah: Steven L. Shields, 1982.

Shipps, Jan and John W. Welch, eds. *The Journals of William E. McLellin: 1831-1836.* Provo, Utah: Brigham Young University and Chicago: University of Illinois Press, 1994.

Skinner, Andrew C. "John C. Bennett: For Prophet or Profit?" in *Regional Studies in Latter-day Saint Church History: Illinois.* H. Dean Garrett, ed. Provo, Utah: Department of Church History and Doctrine, Brigham Young University, 1995.

Smith, Andrew F. *The Saintly Scoundrel: The Life and Times of Dr. John Cook Bennett.* Chicago: University of Illinois Press, 1997.

Smith, Eliza R. Snow. *Biography and Family History of Lorenzo Snow.* Photomechanical Reprint of Original 1884 Edition. Salt Lake City: Zion's Book Store, 1975.

Smith, Joseph. *History of the Church of Jesus Christ of Latter-day Saints.* Edited by B. H. Roberts. 2nd ed. revised. 7 volumes. Salt Lake City: The Church of Jesus Christ of Latter-day Saints, 1932–51.

———. *Teachings of the Prophet Joseph Smith.* Selected by Joseph Fielding Smith. Salt Lake City: Deseret Book, 1976.

Smith, Joseph F. *Gospel Doctrine,* 18th printing. Salt Lake City: Deseret Book, 1973.

Smith, Joseph Fielding. *Answers to Gospel Questions*. 5 volumes. Salt Lake City: Deseret Book, 1957–66.

———. *Church History and Modern Revelation*. 4 volumes. Salt Lake City: Deseret News Press, 1946–49.

———. *Doctrines of Salvation*. 3 vols. Compiled by Bruce R. McConkie. Salt Lake City: Bookcraft, 1954–56.

———. *Origin of the Reorganized Church and Question of Succession*. Salt Lake City: Deseret News, 1909.

———. *Take Heed to Yourselves!* Salt Lake City: Deseret Book, 1971.

Snow, Lorenzo. *Teachings of Lorenzo Snow*. Compiled by Clyde J. Williams. Salt Lake City: Bookcraft, 1984.

Strang, James J. *The Diary of James J. Strang*. Deciphered, transcribed, introduced and annotated by Mark A. Strang. East Lansing, Michigan: Michigan State University Press, 1961.

Stuy, Brian H., ed. *Collected Discourses*. 5 volumes. Sandy, UT: B. H. S. Publishing, 1987.

Talmage, James E. *Jesus the Christ*, Thirty-third edition. Salt Lake City: Deseret Book, 1970.

———. *The Great Apostasy*. Salt Lake City: Deseret Book, 1973.

Times and Seasons. 6 vols. Nauvoo, Illinois, November 1839–February 1846.

Top, Brent L., Larry E. Dahl, and Walter D. Bowen. *Follow the Living Prophets*. Salt Lake City: Bookcraft, 1993.

Walker, Ronald W. *Wayward Saints: The Godbeites and Brigham Young*. Chicago: University of Illinois Press, 1998.

Whitney, Orson F. *Life of Heber C. Kimball*, sixth edition. Salt Lake City: Bookcraft, 1975.

Woodford, Robert J. *The Historical Development of the Doctrine and Covenants*. 3 vols. Unpublished dissertation. Provo, Utah: Brigham Young University, 1974.

Woodruff, Wilford. *Wilford Woodruff's Journal: 1833–1898*. Scott G. Kenney, ed. Midvale, Utah: Signature Books, 1983.

Young, Brigham. *Manuscript History of Brigham Young 1801–1844*. Edited by Elden J. Watson. Salt Lake City: Elden J. Watson, 1968.

About the Author

Richard G. Moore grew up in Salem, Utah. After serving as a missionary in Japan, he graduated from Brigham Young University with a bachelor's degree in American history. Richard also received a master's degree in history from BYU and a doctorate in educational administration from the University of the Pacific.

He has been a speaker for Know Your Religion and Education Week. He was a seminary teacher in Arizona and Utah, a Church Educational System coordinator and institute director in northern California, and is currently an institute instructor at the Orem Institute of Religion.

Richard has taught for more than thirty years in the Church Educational System. He and his wife, Lani, have three children: Adam, Travis, and Asia.

0 26575 52118 4